SECOND EDITION

STUDY
skills in English

Michael J. Wallace

CAMBRIDGE
UNIVERSITY PRESS

CAMBRIDGE UNIVERSITY PRESS
Cambridge, New York, Melbourne, Madrid, Cape Town, Singapore, São Paulo

Cambridge University Press
The Edinburgh Building, Cambridge CB2 8RU, UK

www.cambridge.org
Information on this title: www.cambridge.org/9780521533850

First published 2004
3rd printing 2007

Printed in the United Kingdom at the University Press, Cambridge

A catalogue record for this publication is available from the British Library

ISBN 978-0-521-53385-0 paperback

The authors and publishers are grateful for permission to use the copyright materials
appearing in this book, as indicated in the sources and acknowledgements throughout.
If there are errors or omissions the publishers would be pleased to hear and to make
the appropriate correction in future reprints.

Contents

This book is dedicated to the memory of my mother

Acknowledgements

It is impossible for me to list here the names of all the many people who have given me help, encouragement and advice during the writing of this book and its revision and re-writing for this edition. I am thinking in particular of the thousands of international students who, over the years, have been the target population for these materials. For their tolerance and constructive criticism I am very grateful.

I must thank, too, colleagues who have taught these materials and given me the benefit of their feedback, especially Pauline Brown, Bill Cousin, Alex Peden, Jean Petrie, David Sked, Henry Taylor, Bob Thornton, Cynthia Watson and Jim Wight.

Particular thanks to Lionel Jackson and Mary Jackson for their detailed feedback, which has been extremely helpful for this revised edition. Thanks also to the tutors who trialled the revised materials in several different international teaching contexts. Thanks to Pauziah Mat Hassan for her help and encouragement during the revision process.

Thanks also to the library staff at the Holyrood Campus site of Edinburgh University Library: a particular thanks to David Fairgrieve, Site and Services Manager of the Education Library for all his much appreciated help and support.

Special thanks also To Denny Colledge, Information Skills Librarian with Edinburgh University Library, and Steve Scott, Homepage Online Editor with the Web Team at Edinburgh University Library, for sharing some of their expertise with me. Their detailed and helpful input was invaluable in the preparation of Unit 3 (Basic research techniques) and the Appendix on useful study resources. Thanks also to Paul Fegan for his helpful comments.

Thanks to Olwyn Alexander, Aaron Harrison, John Landon, Catherine Maclean and Brendan Wallace for their help with the audio inputs for Unit 2 (Exploiting lectures and similar learning resources). Thanks to Tony Lynch for his advice on the organisation of the audio inputs, and to sound engineer Alan Whyte for his management of the recording.

Thanks to the staff of Cambridge University Press who have seen this book through to the publication stage. A particular thanks to Mickey Bonin for initiating the revised edition and guiding it through its earlier stages, and to Will Capel for completing the process. Thanks also to Gemma Wilkins and Linda Matthews for their help; and also to Hart McLeod for design.

As always, my love and thanks to my wife Eileen for her encouragement and moral support.

In spite of all the help I have received, there are shortcomings which no doubt remain, and for these I take full responsibilty.

To the Student

This book is intended for students who are currently attending a university or college or who hope to begin university or college studies soon. It has been written with students attending a course for developing academic skills in mind, but students studying on their own could use most of it as a self-access text.

If you are studying for a university entrance language test, such as IELTS, you should find many of the tasks in this book highly relevant. However, the book is also intended to take you beyond that stage and on to the stage where you will actually be involved in your degree or higher education studies.

By the time you have finished this book, you should have studied and practised techniques for:

- reading academic texts effectively and efficiently
- taking notes from lectures, books and similar inputs
- doing basic research
- using library and computer-based resources in your studies
- writing academic assignments
- taking part in academic discussions
- presenting at student seminars
- managing your studies, including time-management
- preparing for examinations.

The book also contains some useful checklists, which can be freely photocopied for your future reference.

Note on the second edition
If you have used the original edition of *Study Skills in English*, you will see the following main changes in this new edition.

- The content and example materials have been *comprehensively revised and updated*.
- Developments on the *use of computers for academic study and the internet as a research tool* have been incorporated into the text and student activities.
- An appendix on *useful study resources*, including computer/internet related resources, has been added.
- *Study aids* and *Checklists* of potential use throughout your studies are now featured in the text.

- To facilitate use of the text for self-study purposes, materials previously published separately in a Tutor's Book have been incorporated into this Student's Book, forming *one combined student-friendly text*.

- The book has been re-designed for use in *a range of study contexts* where English is used as a first, second or foreign language.

To the Teacher

Rationale. This book is intended as a *comprehensive guide* to the study skills required by students who are about to embark on a course of Higher education, or who are already enrolled on such a course. It has been designed to be used in a wide range of contexts where English is employed as a medium of instruction, whether as a first language, second language or foreign language.

Approach. The main approach of this text, and what sets it apart from many other general guides to study skills, is that it is *task-based*. Students who use this book will basically learn by doing, i.e. by engaging with a variety of academic tasks and receiving helpful feedback on their efforts. The book has been designed to be used as a class text, but the very full feedback given in the key means that, with the most obvious exception of Unit 5, which is concerned with discussion/seminar techniques, most of the tasks can also be tackled in self-access mode.

One of the features of the book is the presence of *awareness-raising* tasks, intended to make the students more self-aware in terms of their own learning styles and strategies, and also those of their fellow students. Students are introduced to a variety of study strategies and encouraged to experiment with them.

Teaching methodology. The book has been designed to be straightforward in use and, as far as possible, self-explanatory in its requirements. However, as is always the case, adjustments can be made to suit students' level of language competence and academic sophistication. For example, in Unit 2 (Note-taking skills) the audio inputs can be played as many times as may be thought necessary for the students to cope with the demands of the task. It may even be the case that students (or some students) should have sight of audio input transcripts in order to help with the comprehension process. In any case, where they are provided, the "lecture handouts" should be exploited to the maximum as this is a useful real-life study skill.

The units can be studied in any order, except that Units 4 and 5 (Writing skills/Learning through discussions) assume some knowledge of the techniques described and practised in Unit 3 (Basic research techniques).

Certain parts of the book can be freely photocopied in order to facilitate the teaching/learning process and also for use by students in their future studies. The sections available for free photocopying have been clearly marked.

In order to facilitate the use of the text for self-study purposes, material previously published in the form of a Tutor's Book has been incorporated into this text, forming one combined text.

There is an audio CD or audio cassette that goes with the book, which contains spoken inputs for the Unit on note-taking in a variety of native-speaker accents. All the spoken inputs are fully transcribed in an edited, easy-to-read format.

This book is a companion volume to *Study Reading*, *Study Writing*, *Study Listening* and *Study Speaking*, in which those specific topics are explored in greater depth.

UNIT 1 Improving reading efficiency

This unit aims to help you to:

1 read more actively
2 read in a more focused way
3 read in a more time-efficient way
4 read with greater understanding
5 read more critically.

Active reading

Reading with a purpose

Reading plays a key role in almost every course of study. Yet many students do their reading in an unfocused way. This can often lead to poor results. So let us start by trying to clarify our ideas about reading.

TASK 1 Reasons for reading

1 Think of as many reasons for reading a book as you can.
2 Which of them would you describe as academic reasons?
3 Is there any connection between your purpose in reading a book (or an article) and the way that you read it? Should there be?

(For discussion of this task, see Key.)

Predicting: study the title

Using the title

Read the information below and then do Task 2.

The titles of books or articles can be very helpful to you, if you want to read in a more focused and efficient way. Usually, the titles of academic books or articles are factual and informative: they can almost be taken as very brief summaries of the contents of the text. So you can help focus your reading by asking yourself questions like:

- In what way is this text relevant to me, or to what I'm trying to do?
- What sort of questions do I expect this text to answer?

These questions that you ask yourself before you read a text are sometimes called *anticipation questions.*

Titles can be helpful in another way. Sometimes, when you are reading through a bibliography, you have to make a decision, on the basis of the title alone, as to whether a book or article is going to be helpful to you. Here, again, you have to ask yourself questions such as those above.

TASK 2 **Using titles of texts**

This task practises anticipating the content of a text by reading the title.

1 Choose *three* of the following titles from the journal *Geography* and, for each title, write down two anticipation questions that the article might answer.

   a) 'Global warming and extreme weather: a cautionary note.' (By Greg O'Hare. *Geography*, Vol. 84(1), Jan. 1999, pp 87–91.)

   b) 'Six billion and counting: trends and prospects for global population at the beginning of the twenty-first century.' (By Hazel Barrett. *Geography*, Vol. 85(2), April 2000, pp 107–120.)

   c) 'Unconstrained growth: the development of a Spanish tourist resort.' (By John Pollard and Rafael Dominguez Rodriguez. *Geography*, Vol. 80(1), Jan. 1995, pp 33–44.)

   d) 'Age concern? The geography of a greying Europe.' (By Stephen Jackson. *Geography*, Vol. 85(4), October 2000, pp 366–369.)

   e) 'Changing responses to water resource problems in England and Wales.' (By Rick Cryer. *Geography*, Vol. 80(1), Jan. 1995, pp 45–57.)

2 If you are in a group, compare your anticipation questions. How much overlap was there in the kind of information the members of the group expected?

3 Now look at the outline summaries of the articles in the Key. How good were you, individually or as a group, at anticipating the sort of information the articles would contain?

Skimming, scanning and searching

- Efficient readers do not always read every word. To save time, they use techniques like skimming, scanning and searching.

- When we *skim* through a text, we are reading it quickly to get an overall impression of the text.

- When we are *scanning* or *searching* a text we are looking for specific information which we know, or suspect, is there.

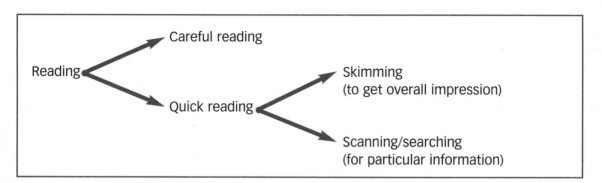

Figure 1.1 Reading strategies [This diagram is based on the analysis of reading processes presented in: Sandy Urquhart and Cyril Weir (1998) *Reading in a Second Language: Process, Product and Practice* (Longman)]

Skimming

Another useful way of building up anticipation, so that you can ask yourself the right kind of questions, is by *skimming* through the text. Whether the book is a set text or borrowed from a library, think of a it as a *tool for learning* that is supposed to help you to master your subject. In that respect, you may want to know the answers to:

- How useful is this book and in what way? (Evaluation)
- Where is the information I need located in it? (Orientation)

The parts of a book that may be useful for evaluation and orientation

These parts include the:

reviewers' comments (often also found quoted on the book-jacket; but remember, only good reviews will be quoted!)

foreword or preface

contents page

printing history (this shows when the book was first published, reprinted or a new edition issued – usually printed on a page called the *imprint page*, immediately after the title page).

A careful look through the **index** should also tell you a lot about the content of a book – we will be discussing the index in the next section.

TASK 3 Evaluating the potential usefulness of a text

This task gives you some practice in evaluating the possible usefulness of a book and finding your way around it. The extracts on the pages that follow are taken from a book called *The Psychology of Happiness* by Michael Argyle. See if you can use this information to find out more about the book.

1 What is the author's academic position? Is his position relevant to the subject matter of the book?

2 When was the book first published? Has anything been done to update it since then?

3 What audience or audiences does the book seem to be suitable for? Has the author any experience, do you think, of knowing the needs of the possible target audience(s)?

   a) What would you say might be the particular strengths of this book for beginner students of Psychology?

   b) If you were a general reader interested in finding out what you could do to make yourself happier, which chapter(s) might you be tempted to read first?

   c) If you were a student whose major subject was Economics, which chapters do you think you might find especially relevant for you?

The Psychology of Happiness

2nd Edition

Michael Argyle

First edition published 1987
by Methuen & Co. Ltd
First edition reprinted 1989, 1993
by Routledge

Second edition published 2001
by Routledge
27 Church Road, Hove, East Sussex BN3 2FA

Simultaneously published in the USA and Canada
by Taylor & Francis Inc,
29 West 35th Street, New York, NY 10001

Routledge is an imprint of the Taylor and Francis Group

©2001 Michael Argyle

Typeset in Minion by RefineCatch limited, Bungay, Suffolk
Printed and bound in Great Britain by
Biddles Ltd, Guildford and King's Lynn

British Library Cataloguing in Publication Data
A catalogue record for this book is available from the British Library

Library of Congress Cataloging in Publication Data
Argyle, Michael.
 The psychology of happiness/Michael Argyle—2nd ed.
  p. cm.
 Includes bibliographical references and index.
 ISBN 0–415–22664–3 (hbk) —ISBN 0–415–22665–1 (pbk)
 I. Happiness.   I. Title.
BF575.H27 A74 2001
152.4'2—dc21

                                    2001018072

ISBN 0–415–22664–3 (hbk)
ISBN 0–415–22665–1 (pbk)

Preface

The first edition of this book was published in 1987, when the field of happiness research was quite young. Since then it has expanded enormously. A lot of new work has appeared in the journal *Social Indicators Research*, *The Journal of Personality and Social Psychology* and in *Personality and Individual Differences*. Veenhoven produced a reanalysis of surveys from around the world, *Correlates of Happiness* (1994). Kahneman, Diener and Schwarz edited their equally massive *Well-Being: The Foundation of Hedonic Psychology* (1999), in which I have a chapter. Happiness and well-being research is now published mainly in psychological journals. However, economists have also taken an increasing interest in this topic, through their concern with whether money makes people happy, and the effects of unemployment. Governments too have started to take an interest.

Since the first edition of this book I have been carrying out research and writing on some of the central topics of the present book, and this has helped me to rewrite some chapters. During this period I produced books on the *Social Psychology of Work* (2nd edition) (1989), *The Social Psychology of Leisure* (1996) and *Psychology and Religion: An Introduction* (2000).

I have been greatly helped by Peter Hills, Professor Adrian Furnham and Professor Peter Robinson, who read and commented on the whole manuscript. I am indebted to students, especially at Oxford Brookes University, some of whom have done empirical projects in this area. Two conferences have been very useful, one organised by Kahneman at Princeton in connection with the Well-Being book, the other at Nuffield College, organised by Professor Avner Offer and others.

Several libraries have been very helpful, especially the Radcliffe Science Library and the PPE Reading room, New Bodleian at Oxford.

June 2000
Oxford Brookes University

Contents

What is happiness?

Why are some people happier than others?

This new edition of *The Psychology of Happiness* provides a comprehensive and up-to-date account of research into the nature of happiness. Major research developments have occurred since publication of the first edition in 1987 – here they are brought together for the first time, often with surprising conclusions.

Drawing on research from the disciplines of sociology, physiology and economics as well as psychology, Michael Argyle explores the nature of positive and negative emotions, and the psychological and cognitive processes involved in their generation. Accessible and wide-ranging coverage is provided on key issues such as: the measurement and study of happiness; the effect of friendship, marriage and other relationships on positive moods; happiness, mental and physical health; the effects of work, employment and leisure; and the effects of money, class and education. The importance of individual personality traits such as optimism, purpose in life, internal control and having the right kind of goals is also analysed. New to this edition is additional material on national differences, the role of humour, money, and the effect of religion. Are some countries happier than others? This is just one of the controversial issues addressed by the author along the way.

Finally the book discusses the practical application of research in this area, such as how happiness can be enhanced, and the effects of happiness on health, altruism and sociability. This definitive and thought-provoking work will be compulsive reading for students, researchers and the interested general reader.

'This new edition is an excellent updated synthesis of the research in what has been a very successful area of advance in social psychology, due in no small measure to Michael Argyle's own work in the field.' **W. Peter Robinson**, *Professor of Social Psychology, University of Bristol*

'This book is bigger and better than the first edition. The author has definitely kept up with the progress in the field and has summarised it well.' **Adrian Furnham**, *Professor of Psychology, University College London*

'Michael Argyle's book gives an excellent broad overview of the scientific field of subjective well-being – the study of happiness, life satisfaction, and positive affect. Readers will discover many interesting, and even exciting, new facts about happiness. At the same time, this is not a difficult read... Argyle has done an outstanding job of introducing readers to an exciting new scientific field in the study of human behaviour.' **Ed Diener**, *Professor of Psychology, University of Illinois*

Michael Argyle is Emeritus Reader in Social Psychology at Oxford University, a Fellow of Wolfson College and Emeritus Professor of Psychology at Oxford Brookes University. He is the author of many books including: *The Social Psychology of Everyday Life* (1992), *The Psychology of Social Class* (1993), *The Psychology of Money* (1998) and *Psychology and Religion* (1999), all published by Routledge.

1

Using the index

Study the information below and then do Task 4.

The main purpose of an index is to enable you to locate specific information quickly and efficiently.

It can also tell you a lot about the content covered in a book. Sometimes a book will have, for example, a 'subject index' (that is, topics covered) and an 'author index' (that is, the authors of books referred to in the text).

If you cannot find a reference in the index for a particular word or phrase, try thinking of a likely synonym (that is, a word which means the same, or almost the same) or a word that is related in meaning in some other way (for example, if you could not find a reference for **chair**, you could try a more general word like **furniture**, and vice versa).

Abbreviations and unusual words are sometimes used in indexes, such as: the abbreviation **f.** or **ff.**, (sometimes without the full-stop) meaning 'and the pages which follow'; and the Latin word **passim** meaning 'throughout the book/article' or 'throughout the specified section of the book/article'.

TASK 4 Using the index

On the next page, you will find the subject index of *The Psychology of Happiness*. Use the index to answer the following questions.

1 What pages might you refer to if you were interested in the connection between health and happiness?

2 If you were a student of Economics, which pages might you find helpful?

3 Let us suppose you were interested in reading about a possible connection between how much people earn (their earnings) and how happy they are. You will see there is no entry in the index under *earnings*. Can you think of a possible useful synonym?

4 Do you think that people feel happier when it is sunny? Does this book discuss this issue? (You may have to check the index under a related word.)

5 If you were interested in studying possible connections between how happy people are and which countries they come from, which pages might you want to look at?

Subject Index

265

Surveying a text's beginnings and endings

Below are some more tips on how to quickly survey a text.

Read through the following tips – on using first and last chapters and surveying articles and chapters – think about whether they will be useful for you, then do Task 5.

Using first and last chapters of books

We have been looking at some ways in which you can do a quick survey of a book by skimming through it. Other parts of a book worth looking at are the first chapter and the last chapter.

In the first chapter, the author sometimes outlines what topics he is going to deal with in the book, why he is interested in those topics and how he is going to deal with them. This information can give you ideas about how useful the book is going to be to you, and possibly also on which parts of the book you are going to concentrate.

The last chapter is often invaluable for survey purposes, because the writer may summarise his main arguments and list his conclusions. This may sometimes be all you need to know! At the very least, knowing where the author's argument is heading should make it easier for you to understand the book. So make a habit of looking at the last chapter first!

Surveying journal articles and book chapters

- At the beginning of many journal articles, and also occasionally at the beginning of chapters in books, you will find an abstract of the article or chapter. If the abstract has been properly written, it should give a helpful summary of the content of the article/chapter. This is obviously extremely useful, so abstracts should be read very carefully.

- Just as it is useful to look at the beginning and ending of a book, it is also usually helpful to read *the first* and *last paragraphs* in the article or chapter, and for the same reasons.

TASK 5 Predicting and surveying

The title of the next passage is 'Malaria – a new threat'.

1 Malaria has been a threat to humanity for thousands of years, but here it is called a new threat. Have you any ideas to explain the title?

2 Now quickly survey the passage by reading the first and last paragraphs. (These paragraphs have been printed in *italics.*) Then see if you can answer the question: Why does the writer call malaria a new threat? If you are in a group, compare your answers.

3 Read quickly through the whole passage to see if you can find the answers to the questions below. **Time yourself** by noting your starting time and finishing time and checking your reading speed (see the Reading speed chart that follows the Key). Write down your answers to the questions. If you are in a group, compare your answers.

a) What two ways have been tried to prevent the mosquitoes from using their breeding grounds?

b) What ingenious modern method of 'biological engineering' has been used against the mosquito?

c) Can you find three other methods that have been used to combat malaria?

d) What two methods are not as effective as they used to be?

Malaria
— a new threat

Malaria has been the scourge of humanity since the earliest times, and there are ominous signs that it is fighting back against modern science. In this short article, we will be looking at the advances that have been made in the fight against malaria in modern times. We will also be discussing why, in spite of these advances, malaria has still not been eradicated, and in some ways, poses a greater threat to humanity than ever.

The first great breakthrough in the treatment of malaria was the discovery by Sir Ronald Ross, during the period 1895–98, that the disease was transmitted by the female *Anopheles* mosquito. Then Giovanni Grassi worked out the life cycle of the human malaria parasite. With the connection between malaria and the mosquito clearly established, steps could be taken to fight the disease.

One method was to attack the breeding places of the mosquito. It was known that mosquitoes lay their eggs in water. So, in malaria infested areas work was started on draining marshes and stagnant pools, and trying to ensure generally that there were no areas of water where mosquitoes could breed. Where areas of still water could not be drained, they were sometimes covered with oil or detergent, which made them unusable by the mosquitoes.

One of the most interesting methods of preventing mosquitoes from multiplying is to introduce a different variety of mosquito into an area: when the two varieties mate, the females are infertile. This kind of 'biological engineering' has had some limited success in the field, but it is not always possible to reproduce laboratory conditions in real life. Since there are over 2,600 different kinds of mosquitoes, the research problems are enormous.

The most obvious and easiest method of prevention is to use wire screens and mosquito netting to prevent people being bitten. But this may not always be possible in poor areas, and does not help when people are moving about. Then people have to cover up and/or use some kind of protective cream or spray.

A more flexible method is to take preventive drugs such as quinine. This drug was at one time extremely widely used, but during the Second World War most of the supply areas fell to the Japanese and alternative methods had to be found in the West. These drugs proved to be more effective in many ways, and the use of quinine tailed away. Recently, however, there have been indications that certain varieties of malaria germs are becoming more resistant to modern drugs, and quinine is coming into use once more.

At one time it seemed that insecticides, especially DDT, might wipe out malaria completely. One of the most successful DDT campaigns was carried out in India. In 1952, at the beginning of the campaign, seventy-five million Indians a year suffered from malaria. By 1965, the spraying of DDT had reduced the number of cases to 100,000.

However, as with the malaria germ and preventive drugs, there is evidence that mosquitoes are developing resistance to DDT. One of the reasons for this has been the initial success of the operation. People became careless. Also, owing to increases in the price of fuel, poorer counties found it impossible to maintain the eradication programme. The situation now is that malaria is staging a comeback, and there are new breeds of mosquito which are resistant to DDT.

So we see that there are various methods of fighting malaria. They involve: preventing mosquitoes from breeding; preventing mosquitoes from having the opportunity to bite people; using protective drugs; and using insecticides. Dangerous new developments are that some malaria germs are developing a resistance to modern drugs and the mosquitoes themselves are becoming resistant to insecticides.

[622 words]

[**NOTE** This text on Malaria will be referred to elsewhere in this book. You may find it convenient to photocopy it and you have permission to do so.]

Other skimming techniques

- Quickly skim through any titles/subtitles in the text.

- Read text selectively. Pay particular attention to the way the paragraphs begin and end.

- There is the saying 'A picture is worth a thousand words': look out for helpful diagrams that summarise what the writer is saying.

The task which follows relates to an article by David Crystal. I want you to get a general idea of what the author has to say, using (where appropriate) the techniques we have been discussing in this unit.

TASK 6 Skimming

1 The title of the article is 'A Linguistic Revolution: Language and the Internet'. Begin by thinking about the title. What sort of topics do you think the writer will be dealing with?

2 Skim through the article. Then answer this question: What are the *main points that the writer is making about language and the Internet?* (You should come up with at least two.)

3 (*Careful reading*) Now read the article straight through at your normal reading speed (not forgetting to **time yourself**!).

When you have read the passage through see if you can give a more complete answer to question 2 above. Your answer should be in the form of a summary of between 100 and 200 words long. (If you are with a group, compare your summaries.)

A Linguistic Revolution:
Language and the Internet
DAVID CRYSTAL

A linguist cannot help but be impressed by the Internet. It is an extraordinarily diverse medium, holding a mirror up to many sides of our linguistic nature. The World Wide Web, in particular, offers a home to virtually all the styles that have so far developed in the English language-newspapers, scientific reports, bulletins, novels, poems, prayers – you name it, you'll find a page on it. Indeed, it is introducing us to styles of written expression which none of us have ever seen before. It has often been said the Internet is a revolution – yes, indeed, but it is also a linguistic revolution.

The Internet is not a single thing. It consists of several domains – e-mails, the World Wide Web, chatrooms (those which exist in real time and those which do not) and the world of fantasy games. Each offers us possibilities of human communication which I think can genuinely be called revolutionary.

In e-mails, what is revolutionary is not the way some of its users are cavalier about their typing accuracy, permitting misspellings, and omitting capitalization and punctuation. This is a rather minor effect, which rarely interferes with intelligibility. It is patently a special style arising out of the pressures operating on users of the medium, plus a natural desire (especially among younger – or younger-minded – users) to be idiosyncratic and daring. There is nothing truly revolutionary here.

What is revolutionary about e-mails is the way the medium permits what is called *framing*. You receive a message which contains, say, three different points in a single paragraph. You can, if you want, reply to each of these points by taking the paragraph, splitting it up into three parts, and then responding to each part separately, so that the message you send back then looks a bit like a play dialogue. Then, your sender can do the same thing to your responses, and when you get the message back, you see his replies to your replies. You can then send the lot onto someone else for further comments, and when it comes back there are now three voices framed on the screen. And so it can go on – replies within replies within replies – all unified within the same screen typography. There's never been anything like this in the history of human written communication.

The pages of the Web offer a different kind of revolutionary development. The one thing we can say about traditional writing is that it is permanent. You open a book at page 6, close the book, then open it at page 6 again. You expect to see the same thing. You would be more than a little surprised if the page had changed in the interim. But this kind of impermanence is perfectly normal on the Web – where indeed you can see the page changing in front of your eyes. Words appear and disappear, in varying colours. Sentences slide onto the screen and off again. Letters dance before your eyes. The Web is truly part of a new, animated linguistic channel – more dynamic than traditional writing, and more permanent than traditional speech. It is neither speech nor writing. It is a new medium.

Real-time Internet discussion groups – chatrooms – also offer a revolutionary set of possibilities. You see on your screen messages coming in from all over the world. If there are 30 people in the room, then you could be seeing 30 different messages, all making various contributions to the theme, but often clustering into half a dozen or more sub-conversations. It has never been possible before in the history of human communication, to 'listen' to 30 people at once. Now you can. Moreover, you can respond to as many of them as your mental powers and typing speed permit. This too is a revolutionary state of affairs, as far as speech is concerned.

But there is a further reason for the revolutionary status of the Internet – the fact that it offers a home to all languages – as soon as their communities have a functioning computer technology. Its increasingly multilingual character has been the most notable change since it started out – not very long ago – as a totally English medium. By the mid-1990s, a widely-quoted figure was that about 80% of the Internet was in English.

Since then, estimates for English have been steadily falling. Some commentators are now predicting that before long the Web (and the Internet as a whole) will be predominantly *non*-English, as communications infrastructure develops in Europe, Asia, Africa, and South America. A recent Global Reach survey estimated that people's Internet access in non-English-speaking countries increased between 1995 and 2000 from 7 million to 136 million. In 1998, there was another surprise: the number of newly-created Websites not in English passed the total for newly-created Websites that were in English. In certain countries, the local language is already dominant. According to one Japanese Internet author, Yoshi Mikami, 90% of Web pages in Japan are already in Japanese.

My feeling is that the future looks good for Web multilingualism. The Web offers a World Wide Welcome for global linguistic diversity.   [844 words]

[Adapted from David Crystal (2001) *Language and the Internet* (Cambridge: Cambridge University Press). This is a shortened version of an article which first appeared in the *SATEFL Newsletter* 21/2 (Winter, 2001): 5–7.]

Scanning and searching

To remind yourself of the various approaches to reading a text, you may find it helpful to have another look at Figure 1.1. Then study the tips below and apply them to Task 7.

- When you are **scanning** you are usually looking for a particular word or phrase which you believe already exists (or may exist) in the text.

- Sometimes – if you are lucky – the key words you are looking for are signalled in some way, for example by being written in *italics* or in **bold**.

- When you are **searching** a text for particular information, you may not have specific words or phrases to help you. However, you may, as we have seen, sometimes get help from the index, or from the list of contents.

TASK 7   Scanning and searching

Scan and search these three entries taken from the Cambridge Encyclopedia in order to answer the questions that follow. Remember, you don't have to read the whole entry.

1 acupuncture

acupuncture (Lat acus 'needle' + punctura 'piercing') A medical practice known in China for over 3000 years, which has come to attract attention in the West. It consists of the insertion into the skin and underlying tissues of fine needles, usually made of steel, and of varying lengths according to the depth of the target point. The site of insertion of each needle is selected according to the points and meridians related to the tissue or organ believed to be disordered, and several hundred specific points have been identified. Areas which are painful on pressure may also be selected ('trigger point' acupuncture).

Studies are now in progress to establish which disorders benefit from acupuncture, but neuralgia, migraine, sprains, and asthma are claimed to respond, while infectious diseases and tumours are unlikely to do so. It is also employed as an analgesic during surgery in the Far East, where skills in local or general anaesthesia are often not easily available. Today, acupuncture is used widely among the general population in China; equipment can be purchased in shops, and used in the way simple pain killers are employed in the West. The efficacy of the method is now being subjected to statistically-controlled trials, but accounts of successes remain anecdotal. Its mechanism of action is also unknown. In the terms of Chinese philosophy it is believed to restore the balance of the contrasting principles of *yin* and *yang*, and the flow of Qi in hypothetical channels of the body (*meridians*). Research has shown that brain tissue contains morphine-like substances called *endorphins*, which may be released in increased amounts when deep sensory nerves are stimulated by injury near the body surfaces. A possible mode of action therefore is that these substances are released by acupuncture, and some degree of tranquillity and analgesia is induced. >> alternative medicine; auricular therapy; moxibustion; tradition Chinese medicine; yin and yang

a) (*scanning*) What are endorphins ?

b) (*searching*) Where was acupuncture first used? How long has it been used there?

2 Canary Islands

Canary Islands, Span **Islas Canarias** pop (2000e) 1475000; area 7273 sq km/2807 sq mi. Island archipelago in the Atlantic Ocean, 100 km/60 mi off the NW coast of Africa, W of Morocco and S of Madeira; comprises Tenerife, Comera, La Palma, Hierro, Lanzarote, Fuerteventura, Gran Canaria (Grand Canary), and several uninhabited islands; chief town Las Palmas; volcanic and mountainous, the Pico de Teide rises to 3718 m/12198 ft at the centre of a national park on Tenerife; under the control of Spain, 15th-c; fruit and vegetables grown under irrigation; major tourist area; agriculture, fishing, canning, textiles, leatherwork, footwear, cork, timber, chemical and metal products; the name is explained by the elder Pliny as referring to the many dogs found on Gran Canaria (Lat canis, 'dog'), and has nothing to do with canaries (which were later named after the islands). >> Gran Canaria; las Palmas; Pliny; Spain

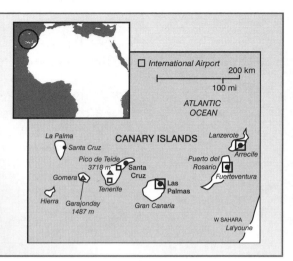

a) (*scanning*) How far are the Canary Islands from the north-west coast of Africa?

b) (*searching*) 'The Canary Islands take their name from the large number of birds of that type that are to be found on the main islands.' True or false?

3 family

family An ambiguous term, referring to both the group formed by a co-resident husband, wife, and children (which sociologists term the nuclear family) or to a wider category of relatives, including non-resident grandparents, uncles, aunts, cousins, etc (the extended family). The nuclear family was once regarded as the key domestic institution of modern Western societies, but marriage has become somewhat less common, and the divorce rate has greatly increased, so that in societies such as contemporary England and the USA the majority of the population no longer lives within a nuclear family group. According to some estimates, only c.20% of all households are made up of nuclear families, the rest being constituted by single parents, foster, childless, or extended families, or simply individuals living alone. For different reasons, the same may have been true of many European peasant communities and in the early industrial cities. In many parts of the world, and in Europe in the pre-industrial period, the nuclear family was commonly part of a larger domestic group including some other relatives and also employees, apprentices, etc. Anthropologists have been particularly interested in the circle of kin beyond the nuclear family, and have demonstrated that kinship groupings wider than the nuclear family may have crucial social functions. >> family reconstitution/therapy; foster care; marriage

a) (*scanning*) What is the difference between a nuclear family and an extended family?

b) (*searching*) Can you give an example of a country where most people used to live in nuclear families, but this is no longer the case? What proportion of the population live in nuclear families now?

[Extracts from: David Crystal (ed.) (2000) *The Cambridge Encyclopedia* (4th edition) (Cambridge: Cambridge University Press)]

Careful reading and finding structure

Using text organisation

Another technique that can help us to understand texts is an awareness of text organisation – the way in which the text is organised or structured.

It is important to know how a text is organised. For example, in a scientific text you will often find the type of basic organisation shown below.

Problem

⇓

Hypothesis

⇓

Experiment

⇓

Results of the experiment

⇓

Conclusions

Being aware of text organisation should make it easier to identify the main ideas in the text, and this is, of course, one of your most important tasks when reading academic texts.

Figure 1.2 shows the text organisation of the passage 'Malaria – a new threat' (Task 5). You will see that it is slightly different from the example we have just given.

Check the text organisation as it is shown here against the original text. If it is possible, you may find this easier if you work in pairs.

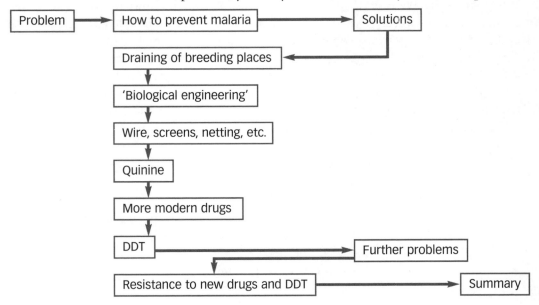

Figure 1.2: Malaria – a new threat

Sometimes you will want to (or be required to) write out the main ideas in the kind of formal summary that you did for Task 6.

More often, though, you will want to record the main ideas in the form of outline notes (sometimes called *linear notes*) which are often more logical, orderly and easy to follow. (For an example of a typical linear outline layout, see Figure 1.3.)

Diagram notes can sometimes be more memorable, and can sometimes make it easier to show how different parts of the passage relate to one another. There are many ways of making diagram notes, partly depending on the kind of text you are making notes on.

One of simplest types of diagrams to use is a branching diagram. There is an example of a typical branching diagram layout in Figure 1.4.

Compare Figure 1.3 and Figure 1.4. What differences do you see? Which of these two methods seems more natural and/or more useful?

TASK 8 Creating diagram and outline notes

Here is a possible summary of the passage you read for Task 6 ('A Linguistic Revolution: Language and the Internet').

The Internet is a linguistic revolution. It consists of several domains, including e-mails, the World Wide Web, chatrooms, and fantasy games. With e-mails, the fact that they are often written in an inaccurate and idiosyncratic way is not truly revolutionary. What is revolutionary is the possibility of framing, which allows internet users to split up messages they receive which can then be sent onto other people and further split up and so on. With regard to Web pages, the revolutionary thing is a kind of writing which is not permanent. Web pages can change in front of your very eyes. Chatrooms offer the possibility of 'listening' and 'speaking' to dozens of people at the same time in a way that has never been possible before. Lastly, another revolution in the Internet is the way it has changed from an English-only medium to a truly multilingual medium.

1 How would you express this information in the form of outline notes? Have a go at it, and compare your notes with others in the group.
   a) Did you use numbers or letters, or a combination of both?
   b) If you used numbers, did you have any particular system of numbering?
   c) Did you use spacing?

2 Now see if you can display the same information in the form of a diagram.

Source details

Topic

First <u>main idea</u>
    (1) Point 1
    (2) Point 2
        - example 1
        - example 2

Second <u>main idea</u>
    (1) Point 1
    (2) Point 2
    (3) Point 3

Third <u>main idea</u>
    - example 1
    - example 2

But
    - exception

Fourth <u>main idea</u>

Figure 1.3: Example of a linear outline layout

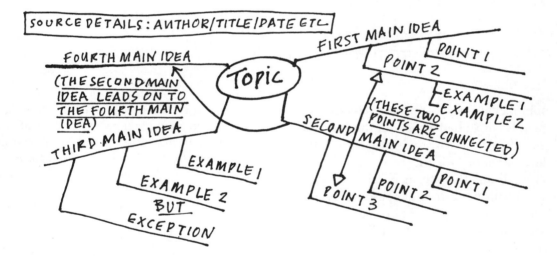

Figure 1.4: Example of a branching diagram layout

TASK 9 Consolidating your reading skills

Now we will attempt to bring together many of the techniques we have been looking at in this unit.

1 *Predicting what is in a text*: Look at the title of the article below ('His Pain, Her Pain…') – and its helpful footnote at the end of the article. What sort of topics do you think the writer will be dealing with? If you are in a group, compare your answers.

2 *Skimming*: Skim through the article and answer this question: What are the main topics that this article is concerned with? (You should come up with at least two.) If you are in a group, compare your answers.

3 *Searching*: See if you can find the answers to the following questions.

   a) What surprising discovery did John Levine make?

   b) Why have the different reactions to drugs on the part of men and women eluded scientists for so long? (3 reasons)

   c) What are the possible biological explanations for the different reactions of men and women to pain? (3 explanations)

4 *Careful reading*:

   a) Read carefully through the passage. **Don't forget to time yourself**. Work out your reading speed by checking the Reading speed chart.

   b) Then make a summary of the passage in the form of either **outline notes** or a **diagram** or both. (If you are in a group, compare your summaries.)

His Pain, Her Pain:

When it comes to hurting, men are from Mars and women are from Venus after all *

Lisa Melton

John Levine was just testing painkillers on people who'd had a wisdom tooth extracted, when he uncovered rather more than he'd bargained for. The women in his study group found that strong painkillers related to morphine, called kappa-opioids, were most effective at numbing pain. But the same drugs didn't work for the men at all. 'In fact, the doses used in the clinical trial made pain worse for men,' says Levine, a clinical neuroscientist from the University of California in San Francisco.

He was shocked. 'The idea that a therapy that had been around for decades could affect men and women in such dramatically different ways was anathema,' he says. 'It was such an incredible mindset in the field of pain, missing what had clearly gone on in front of their eyes for years.'

It is not an effect specific to opioids, either. Another recent study showed that ibuprofen, a widely used anti-inflammatory drug, can be much less effective for women than for men. Researchers at the University of New South Wales found that when they used mild electric shocks to induce pain in healthy young people, only the men got any relief with ibuprofen. It was only a small study, but still worrying, as the drug is often marketed with women in mind.

It's been five years now since Levine first spotted a sex difference, yet we still don't know why it exists. And when it comes to testing or prescribing painkillers, or studying pain, nothing much has changed. Remarkably, even many of those involved in pain research are unaware of these findings. 'I myself have never been able to get relief from ibuprofen and now I understand why', says Marietta Anthony, a pharmacologist at Georgetown General Clinical Research Center.

It's perhaps no surprise that the differences have eluded scientists for so long. Pain is multidimensional and highly subjective, and therefore very difficult to study. It varies with the time of day, age, diet, stress, genetic background and so on.

But not only that. Only 10 years ago, pharmaceutical products were tested almost exclusively on men. Women were left out of the tests in case their inconveniently fluctuating hormones messed up the analysis. Only in 1993 did the US make it a legal requirement for women to be included in clinical trials. According to a recent report, on average, 52 per cent of the subjects in large-scale trials are women. This looks like progress – but it's not. The figure includes women-only studies such as those investigating hormone therapies or drugs to treat breast cancer. And when testing medications for diseases common to both sexes, women's and men's results are often still lumped together, burying any differences in a statistical quagmire.

To Marietta Anthony, who was previously acting deputy director of the Office of Women's Heath at the FDA [Food and Drug Administration], change is imperative. If a drug works differently in men and women this information should be clearly displayed on the label. 'Side effects and efficacy really are different in men and women,' says Anthony. [and] there may be a very fundamental biological reason.'

One of the more obvious biological reasons is that men and women tend to suffer from different disorders, mostly the result of a complex bag of hormones, reproductive status and anatomy. So differences in how women and men report feeling pain have often been dismissed as being solely down to the pain's different origins. But origins aside, there's growing evidence that even when the source is the same, the biochemical signals, nerve connections and the way the brain handles pain are all quite different in the two sexes.

According to Knox Todd, a specialist in the assessment and treatment of pain at Emory University in Atlanta, Georgia, the differences even make their way into the clinic. 'What we see in the emergency department is that males make a public display of stoicism, ask for no pain medication, and keep up a good public front.' But their stoicism evaporates as soon as men leave the hospital to go home, he says.

But who wins in the end? Is having a higher pain threshold good or bad? To women, pain is a wake-up call to sort out the problem before it gets too big. Men, who can put up with more, postpone asking for help until it's too late. Women's prompt action could be at least part of the key to their longer life expectancy.

[740 words]

*Reference to a book by John Gray (1992) *Men are from Mars, Women are from Venus* (New York: HarperCollins). The title implies that men and women are from different planets, i.e. they are very different. [*New Scientist*, 19 January 2002, pp 32–35]

Critical reading

Most people think that effective reading is basically a matter of understanding what the writer is trying to say. This is indeed a necessary first step, but there is more to it than that. The reading process should not be a one-way process, where the reader is passive. Rather it should be an active and critical process.

The first steps to becoming a critical reader

- *Establish your own interim position*: Ask yourself questions like: Have I any views of my own on this topic, and if so what are they? Have I read any other books/articles on this topic and what (in general terms) did they have to say about it?

- *Remember, you may want to change your views* after reading the text!

- *Be at the same time receptive to the author's ideas and also critical of them*, which can be a rather difficult process. One teacher at a prestigious university has stated that his ambition is to produce students who are 'reasonable adventurers', that is students who can be excited by new ideas, but also able to step back from them and assess them in a detached and rational way.

- *Decide how far you agree with a particular expert*: experts often disagree, so you will probably have to agree with one or the other. They can't both be right!

- *Look carefully at the evidence* they bring forward to support their case.

TASK 10 **Multiple reading skills/critical reading**

This task is concerned with practising many of the reading skills we have been discussing, including critical reading. The text is an article from *The Economist* magazine.

1 *Predicting what is in the text*: Study the title [Note: *twain* is an archaic word, meaning 'two'].

   a) What sort of things are economists mostly concerned with?

   b) What sort of things are environmental scientists mostly concerned with?

   c) 'Never the twain shall meet' is a phrase that is often used to mean that two people, or two groups of people, are unlikely ever to come together or agree. Why do you think it might be difficult for economists and environmental scientists to agree?

2 *Establishing your own interim position*: Think of two or three environmental issues that are very important to you (for example, clean air, litter-free streets). Then answer the following questions.

   a) Do you think it is possible to say *in money terms* how much these things are worth?

   b) What percentage of your income would you be prepared to pay to see each of these issues satisfactorily resolved?

3 *Skimming*: Skim quickly through the article. The title asks: *Why do economists and environmental scientists have such a hard time communicating?* What answer does the writer give to this question?

4 *Scanning*: Quickly find the part of the article that refers to a new paper by Professor Philip Graves. What theory does he put forward in that paper?

5 *Careful reading and finding the structure of a text*: Read carefully through the whole paper. Don't forget to **time yourself**. Work out your reading speed by checking the Reading speed chart. Then answer the following questions.

a) This article could be said to have this very common structure:

Problem ⇒ Proposed solution ⇒ Evaluation of the solution.

Very briefly, state: (i) the problem; (ii) the proposed solution; (iii) the writer's evaluation of the solution.

b) Make a summary of the article in the form of either outline notes or a diagram, or try both.

c) If you are in a group, compare your answers to these questions. See if you can agree on the structure and the best summary.

6 *Critical reading*: Now that you have read the article, do you accept that the approaches of economists and environmental scientists are so different that they will never be able to agree? Is there a fundamental conflict between Economics and Environmentalism?

Never the twain shall meet:

Why do economists and environmental scientists have such a hard time communicating?

Academic disciplines are often separated by gulfs of mutual incomprehension, but the deepest and widest may be the one that separates most economists from most environmentalists.

Almost all economists are intellectually committed to the idea that the things people want can be valued in dollars and cents. If this is true, and things such as clean air, stable sea levels, tropical forests and species diversity can be valued that way, then environmental issues submit – or so it is argued – quite readily to the disciplines of economic analysis. Trade-offs can be struck between competing ends, in principle at least, and one can begin to think about how the world's consumption of environmental goods can be optimised, as economists say, subject to the constraint that people cannot have everything they want.

Most environmentalists object to the very first step in the argument – the idea that environmental goods can be reduced, as they would put it, to a cash equivalent. In fact, most environmentalists not only disagree with this idea, they find it morally deplorable. So tempers on both sides start to be lost at the outset.

Ordinary voters are far more likely to agree with environmentalists on this than with the economists. To them it seems absurd and wrong to suppose that a value can be put on, say, the survival of the Indian tiger. Yet the fact remains that choices must be made.

Even if environmentalists ruled the world, choices would have to be confronted – and, working backwards from these choices, made according to whatever criteria, it will always be possible to calculate the economic values that were implicitly attached to different environmental goods. Environmentalist rulers might prefer not to know what these implicit valuations were, but that would not alter the fact that trade-offs, measurable in dollar terms, had been struck.

However, this does not prove that moving from values to policy, as economists prefer, will yield better results than working backwards and deducing (if you care to) values from policy. Suppose that economists are very bad indeed at attaching values to environmental goods. Then it might be better to work the other way round: take a guess at a good policy, and leave the economists to do their (pointless) bookkeeping later.

There is a lively debate in economics about valuing the environment, and some strands of the literature do favour, or at least sympathise with, this environmentalist perspective. For instance a new paper by Philip Graves, a professor at the University of Colorado, suggests that economists systematically undervalue environmental goods, possibly by a lot.

The standard approach to valuing public goods (including environmental goods) goes back to a classic paper by Paul Samuelson in 1954. It says that, in principle, governments should be guided in providing public goods by what people would be willing to spend on them if the goods could be bought in a market. One difficulty is discovering what people would be willing to spend. But that point is old hat [out-of-date]. Mr Graves's idea is that even if you knew how much of their existing incomes people would spend on environmental goods, this would not tell you how much they would spend if they were actually given the choice – because if people could buy environmental goods, they might work harder and earn more, and spend the extra income on them.

Mr Graves guesses that people might work 10% harder on average. (One component of this shift: at least some green activists and drop-outs would get higher-paying jobs, or any jobs, if they could spend their wages on environmental goods.) That number, on which everything depends, looks awfully high. It may seem more plausible in Colorado than it would across the Atlantic in, say, Essex – where if people had an opportunity to trade less environmental protection for extra leisure and private goods, they would probably take it. Still, if Mr Graves were anywhere near right about this figure, the implied undervaluation of environmental goods by standard methods would be quite enormous.

Does this point the way to détente? Probably not. If Mr Graves is right about the theory and in the ball-park with his number, his analysis favours a very large expansion in efforts to improve the environment. Environmentalists would no doubt applaud the result. But Mr Graves is still, deplorably in their view, trying to attach monetary values to things he ought not. Mr Graves's analysis, and other green-friendly work by economists, is still about economic efficiency, about striking a better trade-off – and, in the end, about finding the point at which further spending on the environment would be too much. How many environmentalists can even imagine such a point?   [777 words]

[Source: 'Economics Focus' feature article from *The Economist*, 2 February, 2002, p 82.]

TASK 11 Multiple reading skills/critical reading

This task is also concerned with practising many of the reading skills we have been discussing, again including critical reading. The text is an extract from an article by Lester Brown in *The Ecologist* magazine (not to be confused with *The Economist* magazine, as you will see!).

1 *Prediction*: Study the title. What do you think the writer's argument is going to be?

2 *Establishing your own position*: Do you think that looking after the environment is something that is usually going to cost us money? Or do you believe that looking after the environment could actually generate wealth? Is so, how would the wealth be generated?

3 *Scanning*: Quickly scan through the text to find this information: By what date does Costa Rica plan to shift entirely to renewable energy?

4 *Searching*: Search quickly through the extract to find three examples of countries that have done something to bring about an environmentally sustainable environment. For each country, give one example of something they have done to achieve this aim.

5 *Careful reading*: Read carefully through the whole text. Don't forget to **time yourself**. Work out your speed by checking the Reading speed chart.

   a) The text could be said to have this structure:

   Problem ⇒ Proposed solution ⇒ Examples to support the solution ⇒ Implications of the proposed solution.

   In one sentence for each, state: (i) the problem; (ii) the proposed solution; (iii) the three main areas of the economy that will be affected by the proposed solution.

   b) Make a summary of the extract in the form of either outline notes or a diagram.

6 *Critical reading*: Answer the following questions.

   a) In what ways do the views in this extract contrast with the article from *The Economist* in Task 10?

   b) Which text did you find more persuasive – the one from *The Economist* or the one from *The Ecologist*? Why?

   c) Have your own views been changed by reading this extract from Lester Brown's article in *The Ecologist*?

Extract from
Save the planet (and prosper)

Lester Brown

Today's global economy has been shaped by market forces, not by the principles of ecology. Unfortunately, by failing to reflect the full costs of goods and services, the market provides misleading information to economic decision makers at all levels. This has created a distorted economy that is out of step with the earth's eco-system – an economy that is destroying its natural support systems.

The market does not recognise basic ecological concepts of sustainable yield nor does it respect the balances of nature. For example, it pays no attention to the growing imbalance between carbon emissions and nature's capacity to fix carbon, much less to the role of burning fossil fuels in creating the imbalance. For most economists, a rise in carbon dioxide levels is of little concern. For an ecologist, such a rise – driven by the use of fossils fuels – is a signal to shift to other energy sources in order to avoid rising temperatures, melting ice, and rising sea levels. An eco-economy is one that satisfies our needs without jeopardising the prospects of future generations to meet their needs, as the Brundtland Commission pointed out nearly 15 years ago.

NO SMALL ORDER

Converting our economy into an eco-economy is a monumental undertaking. There is no precedent for transforming an economy shaped largely by market forces into one shaped by principles of ecology.

Although the concept of environmentally sustainable development evolved a quarter-century ago, not one country has a strategy to build an eco-economy – to restore carbon balances, to stabilise population and water tables, and to conserve its forests, soils, and diversity of plant and animal life. Nevertheless, glimpses of the eco-economy are clearly visible in some countries. For example 31 countries in Europe, plus Japan, have stabilised their population size, satisfying one of the most basic conditions of an eco-economy. Europe has stabilised its population within its food-producing capacity, leaving it with an exportable surplus of grain to help fill the deficits in developing countries. Furthermore, China – the world's most populous country – now has lower fertility than the US and is moving towards population stability.

Among countries, Denmark is the eco-economy leader. It has stabilised its population, banned the construction of coal-fired power plants, banned the use of non-refillable beverage containers and is now getting 15 per cent of its energy from wind. In addition, it has restructured its transport network; now 32 per cent of all trips in Copenhagen are on bicycle.

Other countries have also achieved specific goals. A reforestation program in South Korea, begun more than a generation ago, has blanketed the country's hills and mountains with trees. Costa Rica has a plan to shift entirely to renewable energy by 2025. Iceland, working with a consortium of corporations led by Shell and DaimlerChrysler, plans to be the world's first hydrogen-powered economy.

So we can see pieces of the eco-economy emerging, but systemic change requires a fundamental shift in market signals, signals that respect the principles of economic sustainability. Unless we are prepared to shift taxes from income to environmentally destructive activities, such as carbon emissions and the wasteful use of water, we will not succeed in building an eco-economy.

Such an eco-economy will affect every facet of our lives. It will alter how we light our homes, what we eat, where we live, how we use our leisure time, and how many children we have. It will give us a world where we are part of nature, instead of being estranged from it.

RESTRUCTURING THE ECONOMY

An economy that is in sync with [i.e. is in step with/matches] the earth's eco-system will contrast profoundly with the polluting, disruptive, and ultimately self-destructing economy of today – the fossil-fuel-based, automobile-centred, throwaway economy. Among the key economic sectors – energy, materials, and food – the most profound changes will be in energy and materials. It is difficult to imagine a more fundamental sectoral restructuring than in the energy sector as it shifts from oil, coal, and natural gas to wind, solar cells, and geothermal energy.

With materials, the change is not so much in the materials used as in the structure of the sector itself as it shifts from the linear economic model, where materials go from mine or forest to the landfill, to the reuse/recycle model. In this closed-loop system, which emulates nature, recycling industries will largely replace extraction industries.

In the food sector, the big changes are not in structure, but in the way the sector is managed. The challenge here is to better manage natural capital, to stabilise aquifers by increasing water productivity, and to conserve topsoil by altering agricultural practices. And above all else, it means sustaining the rise in land productivity in order to avoid clearing more forests for food production.

No sector of the global economy will be untouched by the Environmental Revolution. In the new economy, some companies will be winners and some will be losers. Those who anticipate the emerging eco-economy and plan for it will be winners. Those who cling to the past risk becoming part of it.

[830 words]

[Edited extract from 'Save the planet (and prosper)' by Lester Brown, *The Ecologist*, Vol. 31, Issue No. 10, Dec 2001/Jan 2002, pp 26–31.]

Note: More detailed approaches to academic reading will be found in Eric H. Glendinning and Beverley Holmstrom, *Study Reading* (2004) (Cambridge: Cambridge University Press).

UNIT 2 Note-taking skills

This unit aims to help you to:

1. take notes from lectures and similar learning resources in an efficient and effective way
2. store notes efficiently
3. exploit your notes for successful study.

Exploiting learning resources

In Unit 1, we looked at one of the most useful resources for learning, namely reading materials, such as books and journal articles. But these are not the only learning resources that are available to students in higher and further education.

TASK 1 **Prioritising learning resources**

Apart from reading materials, what other resources for learning can you think of? Make a list, then see if you can put them in their order of importance for you.

(For discussion of this task, see Key.)

Note-taking

Whatever learning resource you use, you will probably want to note down important points from what you read or hear, either at the time or shortly afterwards. This is why most of this unit will be devoted to discussing efficient and effective ways of taking notes.

TASK 2 **The purpose of note-taking**

Why do we take notes? Is it only as an aid to our memory? Are there other reasons for taking notes? Should we take notes in different ways for different purposes? What use should we make of notes when we have taken them?

(For discussion of this task, see Key.)

Different ways of recording information

There are different ways in which information can be recorded. In the next task some of them will be listed. Make a note of the advantages and disadvantages of each mode.

TASK 3 Modes of recording

Mode of recording	Advantages	Disadvantages
1 Writing down every word from source		
2 Using outline (linear) notes		
3 Using diagrams/branching notes		
4 (Text) Underlining/highlighting in colour		
5 (Text) Computer scanning		
6 (Text) Photocopying		
7 (Text) Making notes in margins		
8 (Spoken input) Audiorecording		

What are your favourite methods? Is there any method you use that has not been listed here?

Efficient note-taking: using symbols and abbreviations

It is usually not necessary, or even useful, to try to record every word that is said – so teaching yourself to write shorthand would probably be a waste of time! Nevertheless, if you are going to take notes efficiently, you will want to save yourself as much writing time as possible, and this is where the use of symbols and abbreviations comes in.

One obvious point, but one that is easy to forget in taking notes under pressure of time, is to use only symbols and abbreviations that you will be able to remember when you come to revising your notes some time later. For example, a student of linguistics would be ill-advised to use phon. as an abbreviation for *phonology*: it could equally well stand for *phonetics*, a related but different area of linguistics.

Study the information box below, then do Tasks 4 and 5.

Symbols and abbreviations

Symbols and abbreviations can be of three kinds:

1 *Field symbols and abbreviations.* The student specialising in a certain field or subject area will learn certain symbols and abbreviations as part of the study of that field. Thus a student of Chemistry will know that C stands for carbon and Ca for calcium. Such symbols/abbreviations are very useful, since they are widely used within each field, and neither ambiguous nor liable to be misunderstood.

2 *Commonly used symbols/abbreviations.* These are symbols/abbreviations in common use or widely understood. Two examples are: 'i.e.' meaning that is; and '=' meaning is equal to, is the same as, means.

3 *Personal symbols/abbreviations used by individual students.* If you find yourself having to frequently note down a certain word or phrase it is sensible to find a quick way to represent it. For example, students of English Literature listening to a lecture on the poet Wordsworth might well use the initial letter 'W' instead of writing out the poet's name in full each time they have to refer to it.

TASK 4 Commonly used symbols and abbreviations

1 Let's start by looking at some common abbreviations derived from Latin. See if you can fill in the blanks.

Abbreviation	Meaning
e.g.	for example
etc.	and so on
cf.	
et al.	
	in the same place (in a book or article)
	note well (something important)
viz.	

2 Now for some very common symbols. See if you can identify a symbol to convey the meaning given. The first one has been done for you.

Meaning	Symbol
is equal to, the same as	=
is not equal to, not the same as	
therefore, thus, so	
because	
plus, and, more	
minus, less, except	
greater than	
less than	
much greater than	
much less than	
at least equal to or greater than	
per cent	
divide, divided by	
multiply, multiplied by	
insert (something that has been omitted)	
from...to, leads to, results in	

Are there any other symbols you sometimes find useful? If you are in a group, share them with the others.

TASK 5 Taking notes from a text

1 Here are some notes taken by a student from an encyclopedia article on the pyramids of Ancient Egypt. See if you can write the notes more briefly by, for example, using symbols and abbreviations, and by omitting unnecessary words.

Pyramids

By the word 'pyramid' we usually meant the grave of an Egyptian king of the Old and Middle Kingdoms (that is, from 2680 BC to 1567 BC). The earliest pyramid was built for King Zoser and is called the 'Step Pyramid' because the sides go up in large steps. It is 197 feet (60 metres) high. The largest pyramid ever made is one of a group of three built at Giza, south of Cairo, by the kings of the fourth dynasty, which lasted from 2680 BC to 2565 BC. This pyramid is called the 'Great Pyramid' and was built by King Khufu, whose Greek name is Cheops. The outside of this pyramid consists of more than two million blocks of stone. The average weight of each of these blocks is two and a half tons (2,540 kilogrammes).

If you are working in a group, compare your versions when you finish. Have you been able to pick up any ideas?

2 Here is another exercise on the same lines as the previous one. See if you can be even more concise this time round!

Malta

Malta is comprised of three islands. They are the islands of Malta itself, and the smaller islands of Gozo and Comino. The area of Malta Island is 95 square miles or 246 square kilometres, while Gozo is 26 square miles (67 square kilometres) and Comino is only one square mile in extent (2.7 square kilometres). As at the year 2000, the estimated population of Malta was 383,000. The capital city is Valetta. Valetta has a magnificent harbour. The Maltese have their own language which is mainly derived from Arabic but also contains many Sicilian words. The major industries are tourism and ship repair. Malta is a very important shipping centre for the Mediterranean.

Note-taking equipment

What equipment do you use to take notes? If you are in a group, compare your methods with others'. Then look at the suggestions on the next page.

To some extent, the equipment you use for taking notes is a matter of personal taste, but it is important to think about how you are going to organise your notes before the event rather than afterwards.

- For most people, A4 size paper (210 mm × 297 mm) is the ideal size, especially if you are taking diagram (branching) notes.
- A4 paper can be conveniently stored in an A4 ring-binder to give the maximum flexibility.
- You can use colour-coded index guides to separate and organise your notes. Plastic A4-sized pockets can be used to store handouts or photocopies of articles and so forth.
- Alternatively, a small punch can be used to punch holes in handouts so that they can be filed in the ring-binder.
- Another possibility is to store handouts etc. in cardboard pocket files.
- Highlighter pens can be used to highlight key information in your notes.
- Different colours of highlighters can help you to process a text, e.g. by highlighting different kinds of information or different levels of importance.
- More expensive equipment includes laptop computers and small portable audio-recorders, but remember that it is considered good manners to ask a speaker's permission before recording.

Can you think of any other equipment that might be useful to you?

Prediction/anticipation

In the previous unit on improving reading efficiency, we discussed how useful it can be to try to anticipate or predict what a writer is going to say in an article, book or chapter, using information given in the title, your own background knowledge of the topic and so on. Obviously, the same applies to listening to a lecture or taking part in a seminar, tutorial or discussion. You do not have to spend a lot of time on this procedure. You could even use just the few minutes while the speaker is setting up to think about the topic. This can help a lot in making what you will hear relevant and meaningful to you.

Let us see in the next task how prediction/anticipation could work with lectures.

TASK 6   Using a title to predict likely content

Every year BBC Radio broadcasts a series of lectures called 'The Reith Lectures' which are intended for a wide general audience of people interested in ideas and contemporary issues. In other words, the target audience is expected to be interested in the topics being discussed, but not necessarily to have any specialised knowledge of them. The 2001 Reith Lectures were given by Professor Tom Kirkwood, who is a gerontologist. According to Collins English Dictionary, gerontology can be defined as: 'the scientific study of ageing and the problems associated with elderly people'.

1   The overall title of the series of lectures was:

The End of Age.

What ideas does this give you about what the series was generally about?

2   The title of the first lecture in the series, followed by a quotation from the summary, was:

Brave old world: 'We are programmed for survival'.

What sort of topics would you have expected the talk to cover?

3   The title and a quotation from the summary of the second-last lecture:

Making choices: 'Choices matter to older people'.

What sort of topics would you have expected the talk to cover?

4   The title of the last lecture in the series was:

New directions.

What sort of topics would you have expected the talk to cover?

Discourse markers (the 'signposts')

One of the most useful ways to understand a spoken or written input (source) is to be aware of the way it is *structured* or *organised*. Listening to a lecture, for example, is a bit like finding yourself in an area that is not known to you, but you have to find your way through it. Being aware of the structure of the input is like being given a map of the area – you are much less likely to get lost!

We will be discussing the ways in which inputs are structured later, but we will start at a lower level by looking at *discourse markers*. If the structure is a map, discourse markers are like signposts, which speakers and writers use to point out the direction in which their argument is heading. They serve as signals for the meaning and structure of the lecture, text etc. They tell us how ideas are organised. So it is very important to be on the lookout for them.

Different discourse markers have different functions. Here are some examples. Study them very carefully, then do Tasks 7–10.

Functions of discourse markers

1 The discourse markers may be used for LISTING, for example.

firstly
in the first place
another (issue…)

secondly
my next point is
last/finally

2 They may be used to show the CAUSE AND EFFECT relationship between one idea and another.

so
therefore
thus (we see…)

because
since

3 They can indicate that the speaker is going to illustrate his/her ideas by giving an EXAMPLE.

for instance
for example

let's take…
an example/instance of this (is)

4 They may introduce an idea which runs against what has been said, or is going to be said (CONTRAST).

but
nevertheless
on the other hand
whereas

and yet
although
however
despite

5 They may be used to express a TIME RELATIONSHIP.

then
next
after that

previously
while
when

6 They may be used to indicate how important something is, that is as a mark of EMPHASIS.

It is worth noting…
I would like to direct your attention to…
A key/crucial issue is…

7 They may be used to REPHRASE what has already been said, or to introduce a DEFINITION.

in other words
by this I mean
let me put it this way

to put it another way
that is to say

8 Speakers often have a number of related points to present, so they use discourse markers to show that they are adding another related idea (ADDITION).

in addition
as well
not only…but also

furthermore
I may add that
moreover

9 They may be used to express a CONDITION.

if
unless

assuming that
on condition that

10 A very important kind of discourse marker to look out for is one which shows that the speaker is about to sum up her/his message, or part of it (SUMMARY).

to summarise
if I can just sum up

it amounts to this
what I have been saying is this

the gist/essence/core of my argument is…

Discourse markers (written input)

The next two tasks will give you some practice in identifying discourse markers using written input.

TASK 7 Discourse markers → Functions

In the passage which follows, certain discourse markers have been printed in *italics*. Read through the passage and say what you think the function of the discourse markers are, using the 10-category classification you have just been given in the previous section.

The rise and fall of DDT

At one time hailed as the answer to many diseases, the use of DDT is now banned in many countries. In this passage, Isaac Asimov explains why.

From the time of World War II (1939–45), DDT and other organic insecticides were used in large quantities. Tens of thousands of tons were produced every year. The United States alone spent over a billion dollars for such insecticides in the single year of 1966.

Not only were crops saved *but also* the various insect-spread diseases were all but wiped out. *Since* DDT wiped out mosquitoes and flies, as well as lice, malaria became almost unknown in the United States. Fewer than a hundred cases a year were reported and almost all of those were brought in from other countries.

Yet all this did not represent a happy ending. The use of organic insecticides brought troubles in its train. Sometimes such insecticides didn't work *because* they upset the balance of nature.

For instance, DDT might be fairly deadly to an insect we wanted to kill, but even more deadly to another insect that lived on the first one. Only a few harmful insects survived but their insect enemies were now all dead. In a short time the insects we did not want were more numerous than they were before the use of DDT.

Then, too, organic insecticides didn't kill all species of insects. Some insects had a chemical machinery that wasn't affected by these poisons: they were 'resistant'. It might happen that a resistant insect could do damage to crops but usually didn't because some other insect is more numerous and gets the lion's share of the food.

If DDT killed the damaging insect, but left the resistant insect behind, then the resistant insect could multiply enormously. It then became a great danger and DDT couldn't touch it.

In fact, even among those species of insects that were killed by DDT, there were always a few individuals that differed chemically from the rest and were resistant. They survived when all other individuals were killed. They multiplied and then a whole species of resistant insects came into existence.

Thus, as the years passed, DDT became less effective on the house fly, for instance. Some resistance was reported as early as 1947, and this steadily grew more serious. *Eventually,* almost every species of insect developed resistance, including the body louse that spreads typhus.

Finally, even though organic insecticides were not very poisonous to creatures other than insects, they were not entirely harmless either. If too much insecticide was used, some birds could be poisoned. Fish were particularly easy to kill, and if insecticides were used on water to kill young insects, young fish might also die in great numbers.

[Adapted from *Twentieth Century Discovery* by Isaac Asimov]

Using the list given earlier, give the function of the discourse markers (shown in *italics*) as used in this context. The first one has been done for you.

Discourse marker	Function
From the time	TIME
Not only…but also	
Since	
Yet	
because	
For instance	
Then, too	
If	
Thus	
Eventually	
Finally	
even though	

TASK 8 Functions → Discourse markers

In the last task, the discourse markers were indicated and you had to identify their functions. In the next task, you will be asked to do the reverse: to identify the markers that go with a specified function.

The origin and function of money

The need for money originates from the fact that different people in society produce different things. This means that people depend on each other for goods and services. Let's take the case of a farmer who produces more food than he needs and a carpenter who makes tables and chairs. It will be obvious that unless some means of exchange is found, the farmer will have no furniture and the carpenter will starve! Clearly, the simplest means of exchange will be for them to use barter – in other words, to exchange a certain amount of one kind of goods (let's say flour) for a certain amount of another (tables or chairs, in this case).

Obviously, barter can work as the main means of exchange only in a very simple society. In an advanced society, we cannot go round carrying the things we make or produce in the hope that we will find someone to accept them in exchange for the things we need.

So we need something which will stand for the goods and services that we want to exchange. Hence the origin of money. It follows that anything can act as money or currency, provided that all the people using it agree on its value. We are not surprised to find, therefore, the use of very many different kinds of money in different places at one time or another.

Examples of 'currencies' that have been used in the past are cowrie shells, coconuts and whales' teeth. As one might expect, things used as money should have certain qualities, namely that they should be firstly convenient, secondly durable (that is, long-lasting) and lastly, they should have some rarity value. Thus, we would not expect large stones to be used as money (because they are too inconvenient), nor fruit or plants (because they go bad eventually), nor pebbles (because they are too common). Nevertheless, it is interesting to note that these rules do not work all the time. To take one good example, there is an island in the Pacific Ocean where the people living there used large stone wheels as a currency; sometimes these wheels were as big as twelve feet (3.7 metres) across! They were sometimes stored outside a man's house as a sign of his wealth.

I suppose that what I've been saying amounts to this: money may (as the proverb states) be 'the root of all evil', but no advanced society can function without it.

1 See if you can find:
   a) *one* discourse marker for LISTING
   b) *six* discourse markers for CAUSE AND EFFECT
   c) *two* discourse markers for EXAMPLE
   d) *one* discourse marker for CONTRAST
   e) *one* discourse marker for DEFINITION
   f) *two* discourse markers for CONDITION
   g) *one* discourse marker for SUMMARY.

Discourse markers (spoken input)

In Tasks 9 and 10 which follow, you are going to identify and use discourse markers as a way of taking notes more efficiently.

TASK 9 **Identifying discourse markers from spoken input (1) (*audio input)**

In this task you will be concentrating on the first five functions of discourse markers as we have listed them, namely: 1 LISTING; 2 CAUSE AND EFFECT; 3 EXAMPLE; 4 CONTRAST; 5 TIME RELATIONSHIP.

Listen to the audio input for this task. You will hear two short extracts from lectures. The first extract will give an example of the discourse function LISTING in use, and the second one will give an example of the discourse function CONTRAST. Note the exact words of the discourse markers used for each of these functions. To help you, some information for each input has been given on the following page: the significance of the information should be clearer when you have heard the input.

9.1 Information for LISTING input:
Title: Role stress in organisations
Words/phrases/proper names:
- Charles B Handy
- role stress
- role ambiguity
- evaluated
- scope for advancement.

9.2 Information for CONTRAST input:
Title: Speech and writing
Words/phrases/proper names:
- language communication
- language media
- spoken interaction.

9.3 For each of the following five functions, think about which note-taking strategies (such as symbols, abbreviations, layout, underlining, highlighting and use of capital letters) might be useful to you when taking notes from an input that uses these functions. Put your ideas in the grid below. As an example, some suggestions have been made for the first one, but you may also have other ideas.

Discourse function	Possible note-taking strategy
1 LISTING	Use numbers (1,2,3,...) Take new line for each item in list
2 CAUSE AND EFFECT	
3 EXAMPLE	
4 CONTRAST	
5 TIME RELATIONSHIP	

If you are working in a group, compare your ideas.

9.4 Now listen to the two short extracts again. Listen to each extract and take brief outline notes on what you hear. Remember to use symbols, abbreviations and layout, for example, where you think they will help you.

If you are working in a group, compare your notes.

TASK 10 **Identifying discourse markers from spoken input (2) (*audio input)**

In this task we will be concentrating on the second group of functions of discourse markers as we have listed them, namely:
6 EMPHASIS; 7 REPHRASE/DEFINITION; 8 ADDITION;
9 CONDITION; 10 SUMMARY.

Listen to the audio input for this task. As before, you will hear two short extracts from lectures. The first extract will give an example of the discourse function EMPHASIS in use, and the second one will give an example of the discourse function SUMMARY. Note the exact words of the discourse markers used for each of these functions. To help you, some information for each input is given below.

10.1 Information for EMPHASIS input:
Title: Learning and remembering
Words/phrases/proper names:
- paying attention
- attention is deflected
- crucial issue.

10.2 Information for SUMMARY input:
Title: Emotional intelligence
Words/phrases/proper names:
- academic advancement
- David Goleman
- emotional inadequacy
- Peter Salovey
- delaying gratification
- empathy
- a 'given'
- 'schooling the emotions'
- static and unchanging.

10.3 For each of the five functions, think about which note-taking strategies (such as symbols, abbreviations, layout, underlining, highlighting and use of capital letters) might be useful to you when taking notes from an input that uses these functions. Put your ideas in the grid below. As an example, some suggestions have been made for the first one, but you may also have other ideas.

Discourse function	Possible note-taking strategy
6 EMPHASIS	Use block capitals; Underline; Draw box around point
7 REPHRASE/DEFINITION	
8 ADDITION	
9 CONDITION	
10 SUMMARY	

If you are working in a group, compare your ideas.

10.4 Now listen to the two short extracts again. Listen to each extract and take brief outline notes on what you hear. Remember to use note-taking strategies such as symbols, abbreviations and layout where you think they will help you. If you are working in a group, compare your notes.

Lecture organisation ('the map')

In the last few sections we have been looking at the 'signposts' (discourse markers) that can help to guide us through the unknown territory of a lecture or similar spoken input. Now let us think about the 'map' – the overall organisation of the lecture. Good lecturers will often help us to be aware of the 'map' of their talks.

Read through the following sections on indicators and cues carefully, then do Task 11.

Indicators of lecture organisation

1 A piece of very good advice that is often given to someone who has to give a lecture is:
    Tell them what you are going to tell them.
    Tell them.
    Tell them what you have told them!
In other words, the suggestion is that the lecturer should start with an overview or preliminary summary of the main points of the lecture.
    Then, having thus primed the audience on what to expect, the lecturer should deliver the main body of the lecture
    When this has been done, the lecturer should in the last few minutes review the main points of the lecture in a final summary. Obviously, if the lecturer follows this system of presentation, the first and last sections are extremely helpful to the student.
2 Not all lecturers follow this kind of structure, of course, perhaps unfortunately for their listeners. Some like to begin with an anecdote intended to amuse the audience or catch its interest.
3 Some like to conclude with just one important point that they want their audiences to think about.
4 Others will helpfully show the structure of their talk with an overhead transparency (OHT) or a handout.

Whatever method of presentation is used it is very important for the listener to try to figure out not only what the information is but also how it is organised – this is the 'map' that will guide the student through the 'unknown territory'.

Cues to main points, subordinate points and digressions

1 When you are listening to a spoken input you will, of course, want to concentrate on the main ideas. Usually, speakers will cue (indicate) what their main ideas are. They can do this in various ways.

   a) They can use discourse markers, such as:
   I would like to emphasise …
   The general point you must remember is …
   It is important to note that …
   The next point is crucial to my argument.

   b) They can cue important points by stressing them as they speak, or by repeating them.

   c) Sometimes the speaker's facial expression or gestures will point up the importance of what they are saying.

   d) Sometimes lecturers will write up key points on a visual display, e.g. blackboard, whiteboard, flipchart, OHP (overhead projector) or computer (Powerpoint) display.

2 Often examples and points of lesser importance are also cued, usually by discourse markers, such as:
   I might add …
   Just to illustrate this point …

3 Finally, speakers may sometimes digress, by mentioning things that are not really all that relevant or important. Often this is done deliberately to give more spice, variety or interest to the talk. Digressions can be cued by discourse markers such as:
   By the way, …
   I might note in passing that …

TASK 11 Identifying lecture organisation (*audio input)

You will hear extracts from eight different lectures. Using the grid given on p. 52, for each extract, write down under the *Function* heading, whether you think it is:

- part of an introductory **overview**
- part of a final **review** (final summing up)
- a **main point**
- an **example** or illustration
- a **digression**.

In the next column, under *Discourse marker*, write down the word or phrase used in the extract that has led you to choose that function.

In the final column, under *Worth noting?*, indicate on a scale of 1–5 how likely it is that you would note down the point.

1 = certainly worth noting, 2 = probably worth noting, 3 = perhaps, 4 = probably not, 5 = certainly not.

No.	Function	Discourse marker	Worth noting?
1			
2			
3			
4			
5			
6			
7			
8			

If you are working in a group, compare your decisions under the *Worth noting?* heading. Where there are different decisions, see if you can reach a group consensus. You may find it helpful in your discussion to look at the transcripts of the extracts in the Key section.

Note-taking methods for extended spoken inputs

We have now reached the point in this unit where we can think about taking notes from more extended spoken inputs.

- Can you think of some methods of recording the information you want to refer to again from *written texts*, which you cannot use with *spoken inputs*?
- What are the main differences between taking notes from spoken inputs, as opposed to written inputs?
- Why is having an efficient and effective approach to taking notes from spoken inputs particularly important?

Note-taking from spoken inputs

Note-taking is a very individual thing, and we all have our favourite methods, but, as we have seen in Unit 1, there are two basic approaches that people use (which, of course, can also be combined). These are:

1 the use of linear notes (for an example of linear notes, see Figure 1.3 in Unit 1)
2 the use of diagram notes (A type of diagram notes that is very commonly used is that of branching notes. If you don't already know what branching notes look like, see the example given in Unit 1, Figure 1.4).

In the next two tasks (12 and 13), you are going to use and compare these two different methods of note-taking, so that you can decide which is more suitable for you. Of course, you may also decide that you will use either, depending on the situation.

TASK 12 Note-taking: branching → linear (*audio input)

Read carefully through the passage called The rise and fall of DDT that was used for Task 7 (page 45). Now look at Figure 2.1. In Figure 2.1, notes have been taken from that passage in the form of *branching notes*. Look at these notes and see how the information has been recorded. Then put them to one side. Do not consult them while you are doing this task.

In the audio input, you will hear *The rise and fall of DDT* being read aloud. As you listen to it, take notes, using the linear method.

If you are working in a group, when you have finished, compare your notes with the others'. If you are working on your own, compare your notes with the example notes given in the Key.

Figure 2.1: Diagram (branching) notes

TASK 13 Note-taking: linear → branching (*audio input)

Now look back at the text that we used for Task 8 (The origin and function of money). Read it through carefully.

1 Using the LINEAR note-taking method, make notes on the text: The origin and function of money.

When you have finished, if you are working in a group, compare notes with the other members of the group. If you are working on your own, check it out against the answer for Task 13 Question 1 given in the Key.

2 (*audio input.) Put your linear notes to one side. Do not consult them. Now listen to text, The origin and function of money, being read aloud. As you do so, see if you can take DIAGRAM notes of the text, using the BRANCHING note-taking method.

When you have finished, if you are working in a group, compare notes with the other members of the group. If you are working on your own, check it out against the Key for Task 13 Question 2.

Note-taking: your preferred method

- Now that you have used both the linear method and the diagram (branching) method of taking notes from an audio input, which do you prefer?
- What do you think are the advantages/disadvantages of each: (a) from the point of view of easy note-taking; (b) from the point of view of understanding, remembering and revising the input?
- Do you think that there is no one 'best' method, but that different methods are suitable for different situations? Can you think of different situations where you would have to take notes, and the methods that would be appropriate in those situations?
- Are there any ways in which you think the example notes you have looked at in the Key could be improved?

Note-taking practice

In this final section, you will get the chance to listen to complete talks and to use the complete range of skills that we have been studying in this unit.

For each of the two remaining tasks, you will be asked to take notes from a short talk, roughly 15 minutes in length. These 'mini-lectures' should be a good test of your note-taking skills, since short inputs are in some ways more demanding than long ones – for example, they give you less time to get used to the topic and the lecturer's manner of speaking. However, the strategy for dealing with mini-lectures and full-length lectures is basically the same.

In these final tasks, you can use whatever note-taking method you prefer.

Each task will have four stages.

1 *Pre-listening*: prediction/anticipation
2 *While listening*: looking at the handout/note-taking
3 *Post-listening*: note-taking technique: comparison of notes/ideas for improvement
4 *Critical listening*: reflecting on the lecture content

So you see, the actual business of taking notes while you are listening is only the second stage of what is (or ought to be) a longer process.

TASK 14 Mini-lecture: Learning styles and learning strategies (*audio input)

1 *Pre-listening.* This talk is about how students in higher education learn.

a) Do you think that all students learn in the same way?

b) Do you have preferred places and times for study?

c) How systematic are you about revision, for example?

d) How do you study a book or article? Do you read it carefully through, or do you give it a quick look-over ?

e) Make a list of the ways you like to study: times, places, ambience (for example, do you prefer to study in complete silence, or while listening to music?), and study techniques (e.g. for reading/lectures/revision/examinations).

f) If you are working in a group, compare your list with others.

2 *While listening.* Sometimes speakers give out a handout just before the lecture or during it. Take a few minutes to read over the handout, which the lecturer has given out to go with this lecture (see pages 56–57. Note: the handout has two pages.). Then listen to the lecture and take notes on it.

3 *Post-listening.* If you are working in a group, compare your notes with others' and then with the transcript in the Key. Otherwise, compare directly with the transcript. Any ideas about how your note-taking could have been improved?

4 *Critical listening.*

a) The speaker describes four different learning styles. What are they? Take each style and decide how that particular style applies to you (for example, would you describe yourself as a syllabus-bound student or a syllabus-free student?).

b) Would you describe yourself as mostly a visual learner, an auditory learner or a kinaesthetic learner?

c) In terms of Kolb's Inventory, are you basically a theorist, a pragmatist, an activist or a reflector?

d) What is the most important thing about studying that you have learned from listening to this talk?

Handout
Learning styles and strategies in Higher Education

Types of 'study behaviour':

Syllabus-bound/syllabus-free

Cue-seekers/cue-conscious/cue-deaf

Serialists/holists

Deep processors/surface processors

'Personality types'

Visual learners/auditory learners/kinaesthetic learners

Theorists/pragmatists/activists/reflectors (see diagram)

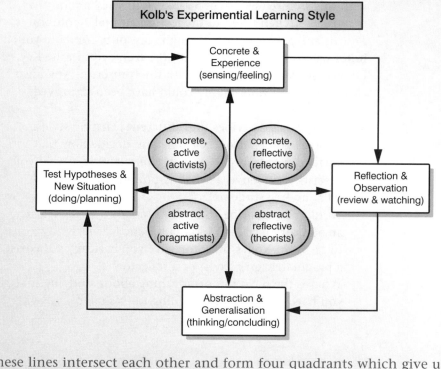

These lines intersect each other and form four quadrants which give us four personal learning styles as shown in the diagram above.

Further reading

Useful overviews will be found in the following.

Clark, D. (2000). *Learning Styles, How we go from the known to the unknown* Online: http://www.nwlink.com/~donclark/hrd/learning/styles,html

Entwistle, N. (1988) *Styles of Learning and Teaching* (London: David Fulton)

Gibbs, G. (ed.) (1994) *Improving Student Learning: Theory and practice* (Oxford: Oxford Centre for Staff Development)

Schmeck, R.M. (ed.) (1988) *Learning Strategies and Learning Styles*. (New York and London: Plenum Press)

References for specific topics

[Syllabus-bound/free]:

Hudson, L. (1968) *Frames of Mind* (London: Methuen)

Parlett, M. (1970) The syllabus-bound student, in L. Hudson (ed.) *The Ecology of Human Intelligence* (London: Penguin Books)

[Field dependent/independent]:

Witkin, H.A., C.A. Moore, D.R. Goodenough and P.W. Cox (1977) Field-dependent and field independent cognitive styles and their educational implications. *Review of Educational Research*, Vol. 47: 1–64

[Serialists/holists]:

Pask, C. and B.C.E. Scott (1972) Learning strategies and individual competence. *International Journal of Man-Machine Studies*, Vol. 4: 217–253

[Deep/surface processors]

Marton, F. and R. Saljö (1976) On qualitative differences in learning 1 – Outcome and process. *British Journal of Educational Psychology*, Vol. 46: 4–11

[Experiential learning style]

Kolb, D.A. (1984) *Experiential learning: Experience as the source of learning and development* (New Jersey: Prentice Hall)

TASK 15 Mini-lecture: Varieties of English (*audio input)

1 *Pre-listening*
   a) How many different kinds of English can you think of?
   b) Have you ever come across a variety (kind) of English that you could not understand, or found very difficult to understand? Why was it difficult for you?

2 *While listening*
   a) Take a few minutes to read over the handout on page 59.
   b) Then listen to the lecture and take notes on it.

3 *Post-listening*
   If you are working in a group, compare your notes with others' and then with the transcript in the Key. Otherwise, compare directly with the transcript. Any ideas about how your note-taking could have been improved?

4 *Critical listening*
   a) Do you think it is good for languages to change over time?
   b) The lecturer has pointed out that there are several 'Standard Englishes'. Do you think it would be better if there was only one Standard English?
   c) The lecturer says that 'you could almost say that knowing a subject means knowing how to use its specialised vocabulary.' Do you agree with that statement? Can you think of any examples where it could be true?
   d) In some countries (e.g. France and Spain) the governments have set up Language Academies which set out rules as to which words and grammatical expression will be acceptable in language use, and which should be banned. Do you think that a Language Academy for English would be a good idea? Assuming it were desirable, what problems do you think would have to be overcome?

(**Note:** More detailed approaches to note-taking from lectures and talks together with further audio inputs will be found in Tony Lynch (2004) *Study Listening* (Cambridge: Cambridge University Press))

Handout
Varieties of English

New words:
    dot-com   cyberstalker   downsize

Shakespeare's language:
    allow (S. = 'approve')   nice (S. = 'foolish')

DIALECT
STANDARD DIALECT
ACCENT

Dialectal variation (examples):
    (UK) Pavement / (US) sidewalk
    (UK, NZ) Go like a bomb / (Canada, US) bomb

STYLE
    formal/informal

Literary language (poetry):
    rhyme rhythm simile metaphor alliteration

Academic English
Impersonal/passive:
    It was found that X happened

Hedging/qualifying expressions:
    It may well be the case that…
    According to these data….
    It seems likely that…

UNIT 3 Basic research techniques

This unit aims to help you to:

1. prepare for researching a topic
2. identify appropriate resources
3. use library resources effectively for research
4. use electronic (computer-based) search techniques
5. log (record) sources on cards and/or electronically
6. use online and offline reference facilities
7. quote and summarise sources as appropriate
8. avoid unintentional plagiarism.

Introduction to basic research techniques

In most higher education courses you will be expected to do more than simply learn the information given to you by your teacher or presented in a coursebook. You will also be expected to find out things through your own research. In this unit, we will be discussing some basic research techniques, by which I mean finding, logging (recording) and exploiting information to be found in sources available in libraries and elsewhere (for example, on the Internet). It is also possible, of course, to do research by generating your own research data (by using questionnaires or performing experiments, for example), but these more advanced techniques fall outside the scope of this unit.

First thoughts (brainstorming)

TASK 1 Preparing to research a topic (1)

When you come to research a topic, there are two possibilities that will be dealt with here:

- you know nothing whatsoever about the topic
- you know something about the topic, but you would like to know more.

In either case, before you start your research, you will probably find it useful to brainstorm either questions that you would like answers to, or ideas/subtopics that you would like to follow up.

1 Let's imagine, for example, that you have to write an essay on the subject of *The influence of television on children*. Briefly (in not more than 10 minutes) discuss this topic in your group and note down any ideas that occur to you.

2 Compare the points you have noted down with the branching diagram in Figure 3.1. Did you have all those points? Did you have any points that are not noted in Figure 3.1?

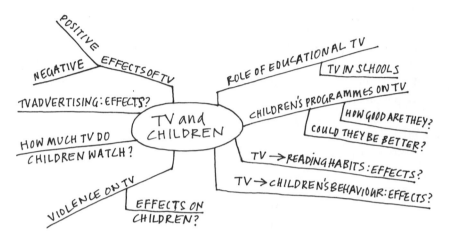

Figure 3.1 The influence of television on children

TASK 2 Preparing to research a topic

1 Now try the 'brainstorming' technique for yourself. Choose one of the following topics and briefly discuss it in your group. Then jot down your questions and first thoughts in the form of a branching diagram.

- The teaching of history in schools.
- The usefulness of aid to developing countries.
- The issues raised by an expanding world population.
- Equality of wealth in society.

2 Compare your questions/ideas with those generated by other members of the group.

3 Now think of any topic that interests you, or any topic that you might have to deal with in your studies, and do a similar brainstorming exercise.

Sources of information

Having brainstormed some questions or ideas, you now have the next problem: where are you going to find the information that will help you to answer these questions or follow up on these ideas?

Read through the suggestions below, then do Task 3.

Possible sources of information

The golden rule for finding sources is to start 'close to home'. The closer your sources are to your tutor and your course, the more likely they are to be relevant. Here are some possible sources of information, in preferred order:

- your tutor (lecture notes, suggestions, booklists, etc.)
- your course textbooks
- bibliographies and lists of references in your course textbooks
- other students in your class
- books related to your subject in the college or university library
- bibliographies and references in books related to your subject
- articles in library journals related to your subject
- bibliographies, references in articles related to your subject
- periodicals indexes
- subject bibliographies
- using databases/information services available through your college or university
- using the resources of the Internet/the World Wide Web.

TASK 3 Identifying appropriate resources

1 Go back over each of the questions/ideas you came up with in Task 2. Which of the sources just listed above do you think might be of help with each question/idea? Which do you think would be of most help? Which would you turn to first? (If you don't understand some of the bullet points, don't worry – just put them to one side for now. We'll be coming back to them later.)

2 Are there any sources of information that have not been listed here that you think might be of help to you?

Keywords and subject indexes/guides

If you know the title of a book or article you are looking for, or the name(s) of the author(s), or preferably both, then finding your source should not be difficult.

Often, though, all you know is the topic you are interested in. In that case you may have to use **keywords** to help you with your search. (Note: you will sometimes see *keyword* written with a hyphen: *key-word*, or sometimes as two separate words: *key word*.)

Another way of homing in on your topic is by using a **subject index**, sometimes called subject guides. These are classifying systems used by all libraries and some computer-based search systems. The most famous classifying systems used by libraries are the Dewey Decimal System and the Library of Congress System. You can start with the most general category and work your way down to the most specific, or vice versa; or you can start somewhere in between and work in either direction. A sequence might be: science > physical science > cognitive science > computers > computers and education.

There are some useful web sites that can help you with searching for information – see the Appendix at the end of this book on 'Some useful study resources' under the section entitled 'Internet research guides'.

Read the next two sections (Using keywords and the Keywords troubleshooting checklist) and then do the task that follows.

Using keywords

Variants: Truncation

Let us imagine that you are interested in the topic: *how computers are used in education.* The keywords here are obviously **computers** and **education**. But what about using *variants* of the words **computer** and **education**? Or **computing** and **education**?

Some library catalogues get round this problem by allowing you to type in *truncated* words: so typing in **compu*** will get you sources containing **computer**, **computers** and **computing**. The search may also, of course, get you words you do not want like **computation** (calculation with numbers)!

Characters used for truncation are called 'wild cards', Typically these are **?** or *****

Scope: Thesaurus

Let us think now about **education**. This is a very wide term. Perhaps you are really just interested in a narrower scope of enquiry such as **universities** or **schools**.

Or perhaps the term is too narrow. Are you interested only in **computers**? What about **information technology,** which includes other ways of communicating and getting information? So you may want to think of other terms that mean more or less the same (that is, synonyms), or terms which include the first term you thought of (**information technology** → **computers**), or terms which are a part of the term you first thought of (**universities** ← **education**).

A book which lists words that are related in meaning in these ways is called a *thesaurus*, and this term is often used in library catalogues for the process that has just been described.

Scope: Refining your research

Another way of expanding or contracting the scope of your enquiry is by using *search terms.* There are several different systems but most of them are based on the *Boolean* [pronounced /ˈbuːliən/] system, though they may use different search terms. This system is named after an English mathematician called George Boole.

It uses three basic search terms:

- OR This is the broadest one, as **computers OR education** will bring up every source containing either of these words – probably thousands!
- AND Sources have to contain all the terms joined by AND – **computers AND education** will have to contain both these terms.
- NOT This is used to narrow the search by excluding search items, for example **computers AND education NOT primary education**.

Some systems use mathematical signs instead of words, with addition signs replacing 'AND' and minus signs replacing 'NOT', like this:

- + computers + education
- – primary schools.

Another commonly used search term is quotation marks (" ") to mean "these exact words in this order must appear in the source", for example:

- **"computers and education".**

Be alert to national differences, e.g. between UK and US spelling (UK colour/US color; UK standardise/US standardize etc.); or the different use of terms (UK primary education/US elementary education).

Keywords: Troubleshooting checklist

Common problems using keywords are: too many 'hits' (sources found); too few hits; irrelevant hits.

TOO MANY HITS
- Quickly sample the hits but don't spend too much time searching through hundreds of hits.
- Use more keywords.
- Use more specific keywords.
- Limit your search (for example by year of publication, type of publication, academic sources only, title, author).
- Use NOT or – (a minus sign) or other methods to exclude unwanted items.
- Use phrases rather than words.
- Use a subject index.

TOO FEW HITS
- Use more inclusive keywords.
- Use synonyms.
- Use truncated forms.
- Use OR as a search term (if possible).
- Widen any search limits (for example, books published more than 10 years ago).
- In your reading, keep an eye open for new sources and use them to widen your search.
- Explore related areas (if researching *education* for example, you might find useful sources in *psychology* or *sociology*).

IRRELEVANT HITS
- Use different keywords.
- Use subject index.
- Look for authors, book titles and so forth that you suspect might be relevant to the topic.
- In your reading keep an eye open for new sources and use them to widen your search.

TASK 4 Using keywords

Look at the following essay titles. What do you think would be useful keywords for researching these topics? Choose one of the topics and see how successful you are in coming up with useful references. You will find it helpful to start with the most general keywords and then narrow your search by using more specific ones.

1 (Geography) Using Amazonia as an example, discuss the social and economic consequences of deforestation.

2 (Economics) Describe some of the problems that are caused for a country by a high rate of economic growth.

3 (Politics) Discuss the ways in which pressure groups can influence political decision-making in a democratic system.

4 (Geography) Using as an example a city located in the 'developed world', explain the reasons for population movement from the city, and what can be done to reverse this trend.

Library search: books

Not so long ago, all library catalogues were card catalogues: that is the details of each book were recorded on an individual card, and these cards were usually arranged in four ways:

- alphabetically by author
- alphabetically by title
- by the shelf mark (The shelf mark refers to the system that the library uses for arranging books on the library shelves.)
- alphabetically by subject.

Nowadays most colleges and universities use computerised catalogues, which basically operate in the same way as card catalogues, but are more convenient to use in many ways. (In many colleges and universities, though, older stock is still only accessible in printed form.) In this unit, we will use examples taken from computerised catalogues.

University library catalogues will have a Homepage. This page serves as a kind of introduction to, or overview of, the library services. Part of the Homepage will allow you to search the library catalogue by clicking on the relevant part of the Homepage. When you click on the catalogue search button, you will probably see a display basically similar to the display in Figure 3.2. Following that, in Figure 3.3, you will see the results that I got when I looked for books relating to the topic of 'The influence of television on children'.

NOTE: for other sources of book details that may be relevant to your studies, see the Appendix: Some useful study resources.

TASK 5   Using library resources

Study Figures 3.2 and 3.3 carefully, then attempt these tasks.

1 Look at Figure 3.2. How many different ways are there to search for a source using this catalogue?

2 Now look at Figure 3.3. While researching the topic of 'The influence of television on young people,' I made a Boolean search (limited to books published within the 10 years before my search) by keying in: 'television' AND 'children'. The Figure shows part of the first page of the resulting display.

a) How many books published within the previous 10 years does the library seem to have on this topic? What do you think are the implications of this result for you as a student?

b) You can ask the computer to sort the books in different ways, e.g. alphabetically by author, alphabetically by title and so on. How have these books been sorted? How useful do you think it is for books to be sorted in this way?

c) Look again at Figure 3.1, which is the outline I generated for the assignment on this topic. Then go through the titles listed here, and then in the box on the left-hand side, indicate whether you think each book would be:

useful (tick [✓]); not useful (cross [✗]); not sure (query [?]).

If you are working in a group, compare your decisions with others' and discuss your choice.

Catalogue

Database | Search | Headings | Titles | User | Login | History | Remote | Help | Bookbag | Saved Searches | Exit

Database: Edinburgh University Library

Simple Search | Search Builder | Course Reserve

Find:

Search by:
Title (Omit "The" & other leading articles)
Author Browse
Subject Browse
Shelfmark
Journal Title (Omit "The" etc.)
Keyword Search with Relevance
Boolean Search (Using AND, OR and NOT)

Quick Limits (optional) - Limit your search to:
Last 10 years, Journals only or E-journals only

None

25 records per page | Search | Reset | Set Limits

| Important information about Setting Limits... | More tips |

SEARCH TIPS

Title Searches

- Omit "The" and other articles from the beginning of titles

  o Sound and the fury NOT The sound and the fury
  o Enfer, c'est les autres NOT L'enfer, c'est les autres

Keyword Search with Relevance

- enter words and/or phrases below;
- use quotes to search phrases: "world wide web"
- use + to mark essential terms: +explorer
- use ? to truncate: compu? --retrieves computability, computational etc.
- Use an exclamation mark (!) before a term to exclude a term: !explorer

Browse Searches

- Omit all punctuation
- Invert author names e.g. smith john
- Truncation on the right is implied: compu
  --retrieves computability, computational, computer etc.

Boolean Search

- use AND, OR, NOT to combine search terms
- use opening and closing parentheses to group search terms
- use ? to truncate: compu? --retrieves computability, computational etc.

More help....

Figure 3.2 Example of a University Library Search Page [© Edinburgh University Library. Downloaded 02.07.04]

Catalogue

Database | Search | Headings | Titles | User | Login | Request | History | Remote | Help | Bookbag | Exit

Database: Edinburgh University Library
SearchRequest: Command="television" AND "children"
Search Results: Displaying 1 to 25 of 38 entries.

FindThis: `"television" AND "c` Find in: `Boolean Search ⬍` QuickLimit: `Last ten years ⬍`

`25 records per page ⬍`   `Search` `Reset`

◀ previous   next ▶

Sort by: `Publish Date Descending ⬍`   `Post Limit`

#	Full Title	Author	Date
☐ [1]	Storykeeping : the story, the child and the word in cultural crisis / Andrew Melrose.	Melrose, Andrew.	2001
	Library Location: New College Library (STANDARD LOAN) Shelfmark BV1534.3 Mel. Status: Not Charged		
☐ [2]	Early childhood television viewing and adolescent behaviour : the recontact study / Daniel R. Anderson...[et al.] ; with commentary by Reed Larson.		2001
	Library Location: Main Library (STANDARD LOAN) Shelfmark HQ784.T4 Ear. Status: Not Charged		
☐ [3]	Keeping the story alive : the vision behind The storykeepers / Brian Brown.	Brown, Brian.	2000
	Library Location: New College Library (STANDARD LOAN) Shelfmark BV656.3 Bro. Status: Not Charged		
☐ [4]	Advertising to children : concepts and controversies / M. Carole Macklin, Les Carlson, editors.		1999
	Library Location: Main Library (STANDARD LOAN) Shelfmark HQ784.T4 Adv. Status: Not Charged		
☐ [5]	Young children's literacy development and the role of televisual texts / Naima Browne.	Browne, Naima.	1999
	Library Location: Moray House Library - Lending Shelfmark 372.6 BRO Status: Not Charged		
☐ [6]	Media addiction : children and education / Alan Storkey.	Storkey, Alan.	1999
	Library Location: New College Library (STANDARD LOAN) Shelfmark pXY 85 STO Status: Not Charged		
☐ [7]	Children and television / edited by Amy B. Jordan and Kathleen Hall Jamieson.		1998
	Library Location: New College Library (STANDARD LOAN) Shelfmarks XY 85 CHI Status: Not Charged		
☐ [8]	Wired-up : young people and the electronic media / edited by Sue Howard.		1998
	Library Location: New College Library (STANDARD LOAN) Shelfmark HQ784.M3 Wir. Status: Overdue		
☐ [9]	Emulation, fears and understanding : a review of recent research on children and television advertising ; a report for the ITC / by Brian Young.	Young, Brian.	1998
	Library Location: New College Library (STANDARD LOAN) Shelfmark pfXY 85 YOU Status: Charged		

Figure 3.3 Example page from a Boolean search request. [© Edinburgh University Library. Downloaded 05.08.03]

Journals and other sources

Study the information given in this section and then do Task 6.

Much relevant (and also more up-to-date) material will be found, not in books, but in articles found in journals and other sources. Journals can also be referred to as 'periodicals' or 'serials'. (Note that an increasing number of journals ['e-journals'] and other publications are now available electronically, over the Internet, and some journals are only available in this way.)

How can you track down articles relevant to your research topic?

There are three useful kinds of sources.

1 *Academic Journals.* Remember the advice about starting 'close to home'! You should explore the periodicals' shelves of your university library and familiarise yourself with the journals there that relate to your subject.

2 *Indexes.* Indexes list the title, author and publication details of articles published in certain areas. The *British Humanities Index*, for example, covers over 300 British journals and newspapers in areas such as art, literature, politics, and the environment.

3 *Abstracts.* In addition to the details given in an index, an abstracting publication will also give a summary of the content of the source. *Dissertation Abstracts International*, for example, gives quite full summaries of theses and dissertations that have been written by students for higher degrees.

These sources can be located:

- in the university library in hardcopy or on CD-ROM. But note that many such sources are now also (sometimes only) available electronically
- through the university library Homepage, which may lead you to Databases, which bring together a variety of sources
- by using a search engine, such as Google (see p. 69)
- by using an Internet universal subject guide such as Yahoo! (see Appendix)
- by using an Internet 'virtual library' such as the Internet Public Library (see Appendix)
- if you know the name of an author, by going to his or her web site. Some authors' web sites will allow you to download their publications free of charge.

WARNING: be careful about using Internet resources. Not all of them are reliable academic sources.

Search engines: Google

As noted on p. 68, there are many search engines. We will take as an example one of the most popular: Google (http://www.google.com)

- You simply type in keywords for the information you need. For example, if you were interested in the usefulness of wind farms, you could type in *usefulness wind farms* which brings up the information shown in Figure 3.4

- Your first attempt will probably bring in too many 'hits' (sources) for you to handle (6,320 in this case). In which case you have to be more specific, by, for example, specifying a region: *usefulness wind farms Australia* reduces the number of hits to 778.

- If you want to make sure that you access an academic source, you could try adding the domain name for educational institutions, for example site:ac.uk limits the search to UK universities. Typing *usefulness wind farms site:ac.uk* gives 246 hits.

- If you still have too many hits, you may have to think of other relevant and/or more specific keywords.

- Another way of getting more limited but possibly more relevant hits is to use the Directories tab. This will lead you down through subject headings to a specific topic area, for example *Regional → Oceania → Australia → Science and Environment → Environment.*

- You will find additional useful tips on Google's own Help pages, on http://www.google.com/help/index.html

TASK 6 Using library and computer-based resources

1 Choose EITHER the sample brainstorming chart for Task 1 (Figure 3.1) OR one of the brainstorming charts you produced for Task 2. Study the chart to see how the various sub-topics (branches) relate to one another. For example: are there any topics which overlap? In what way do they overlap?

2 Use the library and/or computer-based resources that are available to you to find out useful sources for the sub-topics in the chart. (See the Appendix for possible databases and the like.) **Note:** if you are working with others on a particular chart, different members of the group can work on different sub-topics. If you are working on your own, choose at least three sub-topics to explore.

3 Make sure you have a copy of the chart on a sheet of A4 paper. When you (either individually or as a group) have found what might be a useful source, make a brief note (first author plus date in brackets, for example M. Adams (1999)) on the relevant branch of the chart. You may find, of course, that one reference covers more than one sub-topic.

4 Either as a group or individually, discuss/think about how you found the references. Make a note of any procedures that seemed especially useful. Then compare your results with the Key.

Google

Web   Images   Groups   News   Froogle   **more »**

usefulness wind farms   [Search]   Advanced Search   Preferences

Web   Results **1 - 10** of about **10,600** for **usefulness**

EREC Brief: **Wind Farms** and **Wind** Farmers
... around the country, and help to boost **farm** and ranching ... to offer green power produced from **wind** and other ... for the accuracy, completeness, or **usefulness** of any ...
www.eere.energy.gov/consumerinfo/refbriefs/ad2.html - 10k - Cached - Similar pages

MCofS; **Wind Farm** Links
... A lack of co-ordination by the Scottish Executive, and an exaggerated belief in the **usefulness** of **wind farms**, is leading to over investment in a single form of ...
www.mountaineering-scotland.org.uk/ **windfarms**/wf_links.html - 16k - 30 Jun 2004 - Cached - Similar pages

Swantech
... industry. "Many operators are learning about the **usefulness** of this technology for true predictive maintenance on **wind farms**. We ...
www.swantech.com/pr_2003_001.html - 16k - Cached - Similar pages

[PDF] SWANTECH's SWAN™ Technology Selected By York WindPower For ...
File Format: PDF/Adobe Acrobat - View as HTML
... industry. "Many operators are learning about the **usefulness** of this technology for true predictive maintenance on **wind farms**. We ...
www.swantech.com/pdf/pdf_YorkWindPower_011203.pdf - Similar pages

Wind - Science & Technology
... at 2 megawatts (MW) and, when fully operational, the **wind farm** will generate ... We assume no legal liability for the accuracy, completeness, or **usefulness** of any ...
www.britainusa.com/science/other_ show.asp?Sarticletype=2&other_ID=583 - 58k - Cached - Similar pages

The Library - **Wind** Power - Schools OnLine
... Write about the size, location and **usefulness** to the local community of the **wind farms** you have "visited". Do the **Wind** Power quiz. ...
sol.ultralab.anglia.ac.uk/ pages/schools_online/science/scinwp.htm - 5k - Cached - Similar pages

Wind Fa
Can your
Find out
www.win

Se

The Library - **Wind** Power - Schools OnLine
... Write about the size, location and **usefulness** to the local community of the **wind farms**
you have "visited". Do the **Wind** Power quiz. ...
sol.ultralab.anglia.ac.uk/ pages/schools_online/science/scinwp.htm - 5k -
Cached - Similar pages

[PDF] Statistical **Wind** Power Forecasting for US **Wind Farms**: Preprint
File Format: PDF/Adobe Acrobat - View as HTML
... This may limit the ability and the **usefulness** of this type of forecasting model, but for small
wind farms that are unable to participate in formal forecasting ...
www.nrel.gov/docs/fy04osti/35087.pdf - Similar pages

[PDF] Short-Term Output Variations in **Wind Farms** - Implications for ...
File Format: PDF/Adobe Acrobat
... liability or responsibility for the accuracy, completeness, or **usefulness** of any ... 1
SHORT-TERM OUTPUT VARIATIONS IN **WIND FARMS**—IMPLICATIONS FOR ANCILLARY
...
www.nrel.gov/docs/fy01osti/29155.pdf - Similar pages
[More results from www.nrel.gov]

[PDF] Renewables Brochure (Page 1)
File Format: PDF/Adobe Acrobat
... These stations helped the company evaluate the **usefulness** of integrating PV systems ...
the program resulting in development of large-scale **wind farms** at Southwest ...
www.aep.com/environmental/ renewables/docs/RenewablesBrochure.pdf - Similar pages

Scottish Parliament - Robin Rigg Offshore **Wind Farm** (Navigation ...
... structure and therefore would not be subject to guidance on the **usefulness** of training ...
on either side of the Solway and slalom race around the **wind farm** pylons ...
www.scottish.parliament.uk/S1/ official_report/cttee/ad-rorig/rr02-0202.htm - 101k -
Cached - Similar pages

Goooooooooogle ▶
Result Page: 1 2 3 4 5 6 7 8 9 10   Next

usefulness wind farms   Search

Search within results | Language Tools | Search Tips | Dissatisfied? Help us improve

Figure 3.4 Search engines: sample page from Google (Downloaded 02.07.04)

Logging sources

When you have found a potentially useful source, it is very important that you log it, so that you will be able to include it in the list of references for your assignment.

Study the information given below, then do Task 7.

You should find out the following as soon as you can.

- Find out how your tutors want you to display references. Most universities have an approved way of displaying references (sometimes called a 'style sheet'), which may be different from the system used in this book.
- Find out if your university has software on its computer systems to help you with references, such as Biblioscape or Endnote (see Appendix for more information on these and similar software reference packages). If you can have access to such facilities you are strongly recommended to take advantage of them.
- Even if you do not have access to such programs, you can still log sources on your computer by simply opening up a file and recording any sources used.

Whether you are logging sources electronically, using a computer, or manually, using pen and paper, the information you want to record is the same in either case.

If you are logging manually, all the sources you have used should be recorded on cards ('*source cards*'). Cards are better than a list of titles on a sheet of paper. It is much easier to keep cards in a particular order (for example an alphabetical order of authors) than to keep changing a list on a sheet of paper. Also, the list of cards can be added to as your reading in the subject increases. The size of card normally used for this purpose is $5'' \times 3''$ (127 mm $\times$ 76 mm).

Below you will find examples of the kind of information a logged source could contain. Sample source cards have been given for the different kinds of sources discussed. (**Note**: A source listed in a List of References is sometimes called a 'bibliographical citation')

Source for a book

- You must record the *author, title, publisher* and *place* and *date of publication*. You should find all this information on the title page and on the reverse of the title page (sometimes called the *imprint* page).
- *Author*. It is a good idea to record the author's name in full, if it is given on the title page: some reference systems require the author's name in full, though others only require initials for the first names. If there is more than one author, record all their

names. Always distinguish the *author* (writer) of a book from the *editor*, who has collected together a number of articles and so forth usually written by other people.

- *Title.* Note that book titles should always either be printed in *italics* or <u>underlined</u>. Always record the full title of a book in your source notes. Academic books very often have sub-titles.
- *Publisher.* Do not confuse the publisher with the printer! The publisher's name is usually printed at the bottom of the title page.
- *Date of publication.* Usually found on the imprint page. Note that a book can be reprinted year after year and these details are often given in the imprint page. Dates of reprints should be ignored. However, if it is a *new edition* that is a different matter. A new edition is treated as a new book. You should specify which edition you are referring to and note its date of publication.
- *Place of publication.* It is also useful to record the *city* where the book was published, as this is required in some reference style-sheets. If more than two cities are listed, you can just list the first one.
- You may also find it useful to add one or more *keywords* for future reference.
- You might also find it useful to record on the back of the card the abstract/index/database where you found the reference.

Steven ROSE (1992)

<u>*The Making of Memory*</u>

London: Bantam Press

Keywords: memory/brain physiology

Source for a journal article

- Here you must have all the details which will enable the article to be found quickly and accurately: *full title of the journal, volume number, issue number, date* and *page reference*. (By *issue* we mean the copy of a journal that comes out on a particular date. Issues are collected into *volumes*: usually there is a separate volume for each year.)
- Note that the title of the *article* is sometimes put into single or double quotes but the title of the *journal* is usually in *italics*/<u>underlined</u>.

- With *journals that appear weekly* and *newspapers* it is customary to give the *exact date* rather than the issue number.

Rowan E Bedggood and Robin J Pollard (1999)

"Uses and misuses of student opinion surveys in eight Australian universities"

in <u>Australian Journal of Education</u> 43/2: 129–141

Keywords: reliability/student surveys/teacher evaluation/teaching effectiveness/ universities/validity

---

Source for an article/part of a book

- As noted above, be careful to distinguish between the author of the article etc. and the editor of the book. Show the difference by putting 'Ed.' after the editor's name.
- Note, again, that the title of the article is often put in quotes but the title of the book is in *italics*/<u>underlined</u>.

Peter TAYLOR (1994)

"Characteristics of quality learning"

in Peggy NIGHTINGALE and Mike O'NEILL (Eds.)

<u>Achieving Quality in Higher Education</u> (Chapter 4: 53–76)

London: Kogan Page

Keywords: quality/higher education/universities/teaching effectiveness

---

Other sources

Sources can be of many different kinds. If you have not been given guidance on how to refer to a different source, the golden rule is that your readers should be given sufficient information to access that source for themselves. The example is from a journal which can be accessed online. Because web sites can change their content (though this should not be a problem with electronic journals) it is usually recommended that you record the date when you accessed the site. [The word *paradigm* in the title of this article means 'structure, pattern'.]

Yukio YANAGIDA (2000)

"A new paradigm for Japanese legal training and education"

Asian-Pacific Law and Policy Journal 1/1:1–32

Website: <http:www.hawaii.edu/aplpj/>

Accessed: 06.08.03

Key words: Japanese law education/Japanese legal training/Harvard Law School

TASK 7 Logging sources

If you are logging manually, you will need at least three blank source cards.

1 (Book source) If you look at Figures 3.5 and 3.6, you will find extracts from two books. On the left-hand side of each extract you will see the title page of the book. You will notice that not all the information you need for your source card is on the title page. This often happens. On the right-hand side, is the imprint page, which usually follows the title page. The missing information can nearly always be found on this page. To help you, some useful information from the imprint page for the first book (Figure 3.5) has been indicated. Key information for sourcing has been asterisked(*).

   Using the two pages for each book, log sources for the two books.

2 (Journal source) In Figure 3.7, you will see the first page of a journal article. Some useful information from the first page has been indicated. Key information for sourcing has been asterisked(*).

Note: Not all journals are helpful enough to give this information on the first page, as in this example. With some, you will find the journal title, date of publication and issue number at the beginning of the journal. You may also have to note the first and last page numbers of the article by checking them directly.

a) Make up a source card for this article.

b) Read the abstract for the article. Can you think of any useful keywords for this article?

Developing Effective Research Proposals

Keith F Punch

SAGE Publications

London – Thousand Oaks – New Delhi

Figure 3.5 Title/imprint page: Keith F Punch

Name of copyright holder. Also, in this case, * name of author

Date of reprint
(not used in sourcing)

©Keith F Punch 2000
First published 2000, Reprinted 2001

*Date of publication

SAGE Publications Ltd
6 Bonhill Street
London EC2A 4PU

SAGE Publications Ltd
2445 Teller Road
Thousand Oaks, California 91320

SAGE Publications India Pvt Ltd
32, M-Block Market
Greater Kailash-I
New Delhi 110 048

*Place of publication
(City only is recorded for sourcing)

British Library Cataloguing in Publication data

A catalogue record for this book is available from the British Library

ISBN number (International Standard Book Number) useful to know when ordering books

ISBN 0 7619 6355 3
ISBN 0 7619 6356 1 (pbk)

ISBN for paperback edition

Library of Congress catalog record available

Typeset by Type study, Scarborough, North Yorkshire
Printed in Great Britain by The Cromwell Press Ltd,
Trowbridge, Wiltshire

DOING YOUR
RESEARCH PROJECT

A guide for first-time researchers
in education and social science

Third edition

JUDITH BELL

Open University Press
Buckingham – Philadelphia

Figure 3.6 Title/imprint page: Judith Bell

Open University Press
Celtic Court
22 Ballmoor
Buckingham MK17 1XW

email: enquiries@openup.co.uk
world wide web: www.openup.co.uk

and 325 Chestnut Street
Philadelphia, PA 19106, USA

First edition published 1987
Reprinted 1993, 1995, 1996, 1997, 1998, 1999

First published in this third edition 1999
Reprinted 2000, 2001, 2002

A catalogue record of this book is available from the British Library

ISBN 0 335 20388 4 (pb)   0 335 20389 2 (hb)

Library of Congress Cataloging-in-Publication Data
Bell, Judith, 1930-
 Doing your research project: a guide for first-time researchers in education and social science/Judith bell. – 3rd ed.   p.   cm.
 ISBN 0-335-20389-2 (hardcover). – ISBN 0-335-20388-4 (pbk.)
 Includes bibliographical references and index.
 1. Education-Research.   2. Education-Research-Methodology.
3. Social sciences-Research.   4. Social sciences-Research-Methodology.   5. Independent study.   I. title.
LB1028B394   1999
370'.7.2-dc21   99-17596 CIP

Typeset by Type Study, Scarborough, North Yorkshire
Printed in Great Britain by St Edmundsbury Press Ltd, Bury St Edmunds, Suffolk

*Journal Title, year of issue, page references for complete article

Copyright holder

Journal web site

British Journal of Psychology (2003), 94, 175-188
©2003 The British Psychological Society
www.bps.org.uk

Victimization in the school and the workplace: Are there any links?

*Title of Article

*Names of authors

Peter K. Smith[1]*, Monika Singer[1], Helge Hoel[2] and Cary L. Cooper[2]

[1]Goldsmiths College, University of London, UK
[2]University of Manchester Institute of Science and Technology, UK

Abstract

We examine whether reported roles in school bullying, and victimization in the workplace, are connected; the influence of victim coping strategies at school; and sex differences. A questionnaire was completed by 5,288 adults from various workplace venues in Great Britain. We analysed two questions on school experience (participant role; coping strategies if bullied) and questions on workplace bullying (experiences of being bullied). We found a significant relationship between reported roles in school bullying, and experience of workplace victimization. The highest risk of workplace victimization was for those who were both bullies and victims at school (bully/victims), followed by those who were only victims. An analysis of relative risk of workplace bullying, given being a victim at school plus using various coping strategies, revealed an increased risk for the strategies 'tried to make fun of it', and 'did not really cope'. Women were at slightly higher risk of getting bullied at work, but there were no interactions with roles at school, and only one interaction with coping strategies. This is the first study to report an association between school and workplace bullying. Victims at school are more at risk of workplace victimization, but the especial risk for 'bully/victims' supports other indications that this particular category of school pupils should be a focus of concern. The findings also suggest that school pupils who consistently cannot cope with bullying, or try to make fun of the bullying, are more at risk for later problems in the workplace. However, associations are modest; many victims of school bullying are not being victimized in later life, and the results also suggest important contextual or environmental effects on risks of victimization.

Over the last two decades, there has been a large expansion of research into school bullying. Accumulated evidence of the negative consequences for victims and indeed all those involved in bullying has led to actions to tackle school bullying, either at local or national level, in many countries (Smith *et al.*, 1999). More recently, bullying in the workplace has become recognized as

*Requests for reprints should be addressed to Peter K. Smith, Department of Psychology, Goldsmiths College, University of London, New Cross, London SE4 5NW, UK (e-mail: p.smith@gold.ac.uk)

Figure 3.7 First page of journal article

Annotated sources

Sometimes it is a good idea to write a brief summary of a book or article to remind yourself of what it was about.

Look at the following example of an annotated source and then do Task 8. If you are logging manually, you will need at least six blank source cards.

Ken HYLAND (2002)

'Options of identity in academic writing'

ELT Journal 56/4: 351–358

(It is commonly held that all academic writing should be 'impersonal', and that the pronoun 'I' should be avoided at all costs. But there are occasions when this can be carried too far. Students should study writings in their field to see when it is appropriate and useful for the author's presence to be felt.)

TASK 8 Logging sources

1 Take any three books that you have in your possession or that you can obtain from the library. (You can start with this one you are reading now!) Write out annotated sources for the three books you have chosen.

2 Now do the same for three articles. You should take two of the articles from two different journals. Take the third article from a book that is a collection of articles.

Exploiting sources

The usual reason for logging a source is because you intend to exploit it – there is something about the source that you think will be useful to you in your studies. Often you will want to record this by making a source note. Again, this can be done *electronically* or *manually*.

Electronically. If you have access to a word processor, especially if it is a laptop, it may be possible for you to type your source notes directly on to it, and file them as appropriate.

Manually. It is often more convenient to make source notes manually. As with logging sources, the best method if you are making source notes from many different sources is to use cards (notecards). This is because you will probably want to rearrange the source notes when you come to write your essay, and it is usually easier to do this if they are written on cards.

Source notes can take the form of:
- a direct quotation from a source
- a summary of the source or a particular section of the source
- your comments on, or reactions to, the source.

In order to avoid PLAGIARISM (discussed in more detail at the end of this unit):
- take great care to distinguish between: a) your own words and words that you are quoting from a source; and b) your own comments/ideas and the ideas that you have taken from your source
- make the distinction clear by (for example) using different coloured inks for quotations/source ideas/your own ideas, by highlighting using different colours, underlining or drawing a box round your own thoughts/comments/ideas.

TASK 9 Quoting and summarising (1)

Study the example source notes **A** and **B** below.
1 What differences do you notice between them?
2 What are the advantages/disadvantages of each way of using a source?

Source note **A**

In surveying the reasons behind the comparative wealth of some nations and the comparative poverty of others, David Landes (1999) highlights the importance of cultural factors in economic development, but points out that there are many other factors at work as well: there is no one simple solution to economic progress. He concludes by emphasising the importance of generally having a positive attitude, even though this may not always be justified.

Source: David S Landes (1999) The Wealth and Poverty of Nations.

London: Abacus

Source note **B**

After surveying the many factors that contribute to economic development, David Landes concludes with this thought:

"In this world, the optimists have it, not because they are always right, but because they are positive. (...)

Educated, eyes-open optimism pays; pessimism can only offer the empty consolation of being right."

(Landes, 1999:524)

Source: David S Landes (1999) <u>The Wealth and Poverty of Nations</u>.

London: Abacus

Guidance on quoting
Study the information below, then do Task 10.

Here are some useful rules for quoting from a source.
- Make sure you quote the writer's words exactly.
- Always acknowledge the author when you use someone else's words (or ideas!).
- Indicate an omitted section by using three dots. If the omitted section is quite long, you can indicate this by putting brackets round the dots, thus: (…).

- Anything that you add (to make a reference clearer, for example) should be in square brackets thus: The writer states that 'He [Shakespeare] is as relevant today as he ever was.'
- Extended quotations can be inset from the margin and/or printed in a smaller size of type.
- You don't have to put all the source details on a source note but make sure any source you make notes from has been fully logged somewhere.

TASK 10 Quoting and summarising (2)
Read the extract below and do the tasks that follow it.

Some words or phrases that may cause difficulty are explained under the heading: *Vocabulary*.

Edited extract from: Hazel Muir and Betsy Mason 'Secret lives of dogs' (*New Scientist*, 3 August 2002, p 20).

[*Vocabulary*:
rodents order of mammals that includes rats, mice etc;
primates order of mammals that includes apes and man;
sequence arrangement of things in order, e.g. 1, 2, 3;
surreptitiously secretly]

Animals such as birds and rodents can tell when one pile of objects is bigger than another. But to count, an animal has to recognise that each object in a set corresponds to a single number and that the last number in a sequence represents the total number of objects.

Many primates have this basic mathematical ability. But Robert Young, an animal behaviour expert at the Pontifical Catholic University of Minas Gerais in Belo Horizonte, Brazil, suspected that dogs do too.

To test the idea, Young and his colleague Rebecca West of De Montfort University in Lincoln, England, borrowed a technique that has been used to show that five-month old babies can count. A number of toy dolls are placed in front of a baby and then a screen is raised to hide them. The infant then watches as some dolls are added or taken away before the screen is lowered to reveal the final result. If the experimenter has played a trick and surreptitiously added or taken away a doll, the baby looks at the dolls for much longer, presumably because he or she has done the calculation and the number of dolls contradicts the baby's expectations.

Young and West repeated the experiments on 11 mongrels using bowls of dog food. Sure enough, the dogs stared at the bowls for much longer when the sums didn't add up. Dogs paid little attention when one plus one bowl resulted in two bowls, the researchers will report in an upcoming issue of *Animal Cognition*. But they were confused when the experiment was manipulated to show that one plus one bowl appeared to equal three bowls, for example.

Dogs are descended from wolves, which not only have a large neocortex – the brain's centre of reasoning – but also live in large social groups. So their mathematical ability could, in evolutionary terms, have been useful for working out how many allies and enemies they had in a pack, says Young.

1 Log the source of this extract.
2 Write a one-sentence summary of the main point that this passage is making.
3 Write a quotation from the extract which shows what researchers mean when they say that an animal can 'count'. *Remember that you can omit an irrelevant section (using three dots to show the omission) and you can add information in square brackets to make the meaning clearer.*
4 (Critical reading) Do you agree with Robert Young's theory about the usefulness of 'counting' for dogs' survival? Give your reasons for agreeing or disagreeing with it.

Tips for exploiting sources
Study the information below and then do Task 11.

Rules for exploiting sources
- Always have a reason for using a source, such as any of the following:
  - it supports your argument
  - you want to argue against it
  - it gives a definition that you want to use.
- If you use sources that give different points of view, say which view you agree with and why.
- Don't refer to sources simply to show how much you have read.
- Expect to find that some of the sources you come across will be irrelevant or redundant.
- When writing an assignment, whether you are quoting or summarising, always take care to make it very clear which words or ideas come from a source and which are you own. **Avoid plagiarism**. (Plagiarism will be discussed in the next section.)

TASK 11 Exploiting sources

In the task that follows, you can see how an expert academic writer has used sources.

The extracts which follow are concerned with (1) the problem of how students can become 'addicted' to using computers, and (2) the distinction between being 'addicted' and being simply very interested in computers ('engagement'). By means of a questionnaire/checklist, the researcher analysed the various factors involved in addiction/engagement. He found that standard 'addiction' checklists can be useful, but there is a danger that one can end up overestimating the extent to which 'computer-addiction' exists among students.

The source of the extracts is detailed below. The first extract comes from near the beginning of the article, and the second extract comes near the end of the same article. The sources mentioned in the extracts can be found listed in the answer key for this task. [The full article can be accessed from this site: www.bps.org.uk/publications/journals.cfm]

Note: The first section is divided into two paragraphs (indicated by §1 and §2).

The writer uses some technical language which has been italicised and glossed (explained) in the square brackets that follow.

Do question 1, then read the extracts.

1 *Critical reading: establishing your own interim position*
Do you think it is possible for people to become 'addicted' to using computers in the same way that they can become addicted to gambling, alcohol or drugs? In what ways could becoming too much involved with computers be harmful to a person?

After you have thought about/discussed these questions, read the extracts.

[1] Pathological [harmful] computing behaviours

[§1] Early literature on *over-zealous* [too keen] computing behaviour tended to be *anecdotal* [based on personal stories rather than scientific research] and concentrated on the negative effects of such behaviour, usually exhibited by programmers in *vocational settings* [i.e. when learning how to devise computer programs]. For example, Weinberg (1971) discussed programmers so caught up with programming that they failed to document their work properly, and discussed the problems that this caused with the future maintenance of programs. Similarly, Weizenbaum (1984) contrasted 'compulsive' programmers with professional and dedicated programmers. The latter were said to perceive computer usage as just one stage in the problem-solving process, only interacting with the computer when the problem-solving process demanded it: they saw the computer as a means towards the end of problem-solving. However, compulsive programmers were said to treat problems as a means towards interacting with the computer. Again, such interaction was said to take place at the expense of other important tasks such as documenting and planning. Finally, Kuiper (1992) noted the existence of 'Space Cadets' in commercial and industrial computing departments: individuals who '...spend an incredibly large percentage of their waking hours in front of a computer terminal and have few, if any, other interests or ambitions', viewing their work as '...entertainment' and looking upon their company's computing installation as their '...personal playground.' (quotations from Kuiper. 1992, p 115).

[§2] More recent work has focused upon both *Internet-mediated and non-Internet-mediated computer game playing* [i.e. computer games that are played using the Internet and those that are not] and chat-room dialogues (Griffiths,1997; Griffiths & Hunt,1998; Young 1996b). Here possible over-involvement extends beyond working environments to educational and home environments. For example, expenditure of large amounts of student time, which should be devoted to studying, upon 'surfing' has been judged a cause for concern. Such activities are encouraged by free and easy Internet access within college and by the large amounts of unstructured time students have while at college (Moore,1995 cited by Griffiths, 1998). Thus lecturers at several US universities have expressed concern at student performance and lack of integration as a result of Internet use (Young, 1999). Such concerns have been borne out from a student perspective too, with one survey showing 58% of students as variously reporting a worsening of study habits or grades, absence from classes, or being disciplined because of excessive Internet use (Young, 1996a). Worries that people can become over-involved with the Internet are deepened by longitudinal [long-term] research linking increased use with reduced intra-familial [within the family] communication, decreases in the size of an individual's social networks [meeting with friends etc.], and an increase in loneliness and depression, *albeit that* [although] some of these effects are small (Kraut, Patterson, Lundmark, Kiesler, Mukopadhyay & Scerlis, 1998).

(...)

[2] Conclusion

To conclude, the present work suggests that computer addiction is a *viable psychometric construct* [i.e. it can be measured using psychological tests], and case studies outlined by Griffiths (1998) and Young (1996b) illustrate that, for certain individuals, addiction, by its very definition, constitutes a significant problem. However, it is likely that, in many cases, addiction is confused with *non-pathological high engagement* [harmless enthusiasm], and that the classification procedures are likely to lead to overestimation of the numbers of people addicted to specific computing activities.

(...)

[Extracts from: John P. Charlton (2002) A factor-analytic investigation of computer 'addiction' and engagement. *British Journal of Psychology*, 93(3): 329–344.]

2 *Quoting and summarising sources*

Go through the extracts and highlight, underline or simply make a note of all the sources that are used. Then answer the questions below.

a) In the first paragraph, what purpose do the references to Weinberg (1971), Weizenbaum (1984) and Kuiper (1992) serve?

b) Charlton mostly summarises his sources but in the case of Kuiper (1992) he uses a quotation. Why do you think he makes a point of directly quoting from Kuiper (1992)?

c) As one of his references, Charlton has '(Moore, 1995 cited by Griffiths, 1998)'. (Cited means 'quoted'.) Why does the writer phrase his reference in this way?

d) In the second paragraph, what purpose is served by the references to Young (1999) and Young (1996a)?

e) How far does Charlton (i) agree with his sources and (ii) disagree with or question his sources?

f) Generally, looking at both extracts, what use do you think Charlton makes of his sources?

Plagiarism

Plagiarism has already been referred to in this unit more than once because it is very serious matter. What is plagiarism and how can it be avoided? Read the information below and then do Task 12.

Plagiarism defined

- Basically, plagiarism means presenting someone else's words and ideas as if they were your own.
- It is regarded as a form of cheating and therefore treated very seriously by tutors and examiners.
- Plagiarism can be intentional, as when a student copies another student's work or lifts ready-written essays from an Internet source. When discovered, this kind of behaviour is usually severely punished, and rightly so.
- Plagiarism can sometimes be unintentional, as when students use a writer's words or ideas without proper acknowledgement (that is, without properly recording the source) or simply copy something that has been published without adding anything of their own. This kind of lazy and careless work can also be severely penalised.

TASK 12   Avoiding plagiarism

The purpose of this task is to help you to avoid unintentional plagiarism.

You will find below an original passage, **A**, taken from page 10 of the book:

Francis FUKUYAMA (2003) *Our Posthuman Future: Consequences of the biotechnology revolution.* (London: Profile Books)

This is then followed by three passages, **B** to **D**, in which **A** is plagiarised in various ways. The fourth passage, **E**, shows **A** being exploited in an acceptable way.

Note: By 'biotechnology' Fukuyama means 'the use of techniques to manipulate or change biological processes in human beings, animals or plants in order to achieve some desired result'. In the run-up to this passage, he suggests that as well as these desired results there may be some unwelcome results that may be physical and therefore easily seen (overt) or else spiritual (affecting our minds/souls) and therefore not so easily observed (subtle).

A ORIGINAL PASSAGE

What should we do in response to biotechnology that in the future will mix great potential benefits with threats that are either physical and overt or spiritual and subtle? The answer is obvious. *We should use the power of the state to regulate it.* And if this proves to be beyond the power of any individual nation-state to regulate, it needs to be regulated on an international basis. We need to start thinking concretely now about how to build institutions that can discriminate between good and bad uses of biotechnology, and effectively enforce these rules both nationally and internationally.

1 What do you think the 'threats' of biotechnology might be?
2 Do you agree with Fukuyama's proposal?
3 Whether you agree or not, can you think of any problems that might arise in implementing it?

B PLAGIARISED VERSION 1

In this essay I am going to deal with the question of what should be done to offset the dangers posed by biotechnology. My view is (1) that we should use the power of the state to regulate it; (2) if necessary this should also be done on an international basis. This means that we have to start thinking about how we can build institutions that can discriminate between good and bad uses of biotechnology, and effectively enforce these rules nationally and internationally.

4 In what ways does this passage reveal plagiarism?

C PLAGIARISED VERSION 2

In this essay I am going to deal with the question of what should be done to offset the dangers posed by biotechnology. I agree with Fukuyama (Fukuyama 2003) that *we should use the power of the state to regulate it. And if this proves to be beyond the power of any individual nation-state to regulate, it needs to be regulated on an international basis. We need to start thinking concretely now about how to build institutions that can discriminate between good and bad uses of biotechnology, and effectively enforce these rules both nationally and internationally.*

5 In what ways does this passage reveal plagiarism?

D PLAGIARISED VERSION 3

> In this essay I am going to deal with the question of what should be done to offset the dangers posed by biotechnology. I agree with Fukuyama (Fukuyama 2003:10) when he says that "we should use the power of the state to regulate biotechnology." If individual nation-states can't regulate it, it needs to be regulated on an international basis. We should start thinking now about how to build institutions that can discriminate between good and bad uses of biotechnology, and effectively enforce these rules. That will be the theme of this essay.

6 In what ways does this passage reveal plagiarism?

E ACCEPTABLE VERSION

> In this essay I am going to deal with the question of what should be done to offset the dangers posed by biotechnology. Many people would agree with Francis Fukuyama when he says: "We should use the power of the state to regulate it [biotechnology]." (Fukuyama, 2003:10. Italics in original.) He then goes on to suggest that if this cannot be done on a national basis it could be done internationally. For Fukuyama, this idea of top-down regulation is a key point.
> Regulation is, of course, essential. However, it will be suggested here that, in democratic societies, it is vital that the public has faith in the governmental decision-making process, particularly in view of the economic pressures of globalised commerce on national and international governing bodies. Several examples will be given of cases where there has been a complete breakdown of trust on the part of large sections of the community with regard to official directives on health and safety issues. It will be argued that if we are to combat the dangers posed by biotechnology, there is a clear need for much more transparency in the setting-up and administration of official advisory bodies. The essay will conclude by suggesting ways in which greater transparency might be achieved.

7 Why is this an acceptable example of the use of a source?

UNIT 4 Writing skills

This unit aims to help you to:

1. interpret assignments in terms of topic and frame
2. organise your assignments in an appropriate way
3. use writing techniques that are effective and appropriate
4. prepare assignments for submission (so that they can be marked/evaluated).

Topics and frames

Most assignment titles contain two elements: the *topic* and the *frame*.

- The *topic* relates to the content of what you are going to write. You should make a practice of highlighting keywords in the topic.
- The *frame* tells you how you are supposed to structure/organise the content. It is possible to have much good content in an assignment, but still receive a poor mark because the assignment is not organised in a way that responds to the demands of the frame.

The following example shows the topic in *italics*, with the keywords in CAPITALS; and the frame is printed in **bold**.

The use of VIDEO CAMERAS in PUBLIC PLACES in order to PREVENT CRIME is becoming more WIDESPREAD. **Is this a good thing? Discuss**.

Some possible patterns of assignment organisation are illustrated in Figure 4.1. Examine them carefully and make sure you understand them.

·········

TASK 1 **Topics, frames and assignment organisation**

1 You will find below a selection of assignments relating to different subjects. For each one:
   a) divide the frames from the topics, for example by underlining or highlighting
   b) identify the keywords in the topics
   c) taking each frame in turn, think about/discuss how each frame will affect the way in which the assignment should be organised

d) try to match each frame with the appropriate organisation pattern in Figure 4.1.

Here are the assignments.

Assignment 1   What factors would you identify in explaining why women now make up nearly half of Britain's labour force?

Assignment 2   Why does scholastic achievement at school and university level vary between students from different social classes and ethnic backgrounds?

Assignment 3   What evidence is there either to support or contradict the view that the media have a powerful influence on audience beliefs?

Assignment 4   In what ways are the patterns of immigration into Australia and the United States similar and in what ways are they different?

Assignment 5   Give an account of the legislative procedures by which new laws are enacted at national level in Malaysia.

Assignment 6   Many industrially advanced countries have ageing populations. Should something be done about this and, if so, what?

Some frames considered in detail

Some common frames will be discussed below. (Note: since the organisation of Listing – Pattern **C** – is usually fairly straightforward, it will not be discussed in detail here.)

Frame 1: Process description
Process description involves describing how something works or is organised or arranged. Process description is only possible if you have a clear understanding of the process yourself. If so, the next difficult bit is explaining it clearly for your audience. Often a diagram will be useful.

Figure 4.1 Frames and their organisation patterns

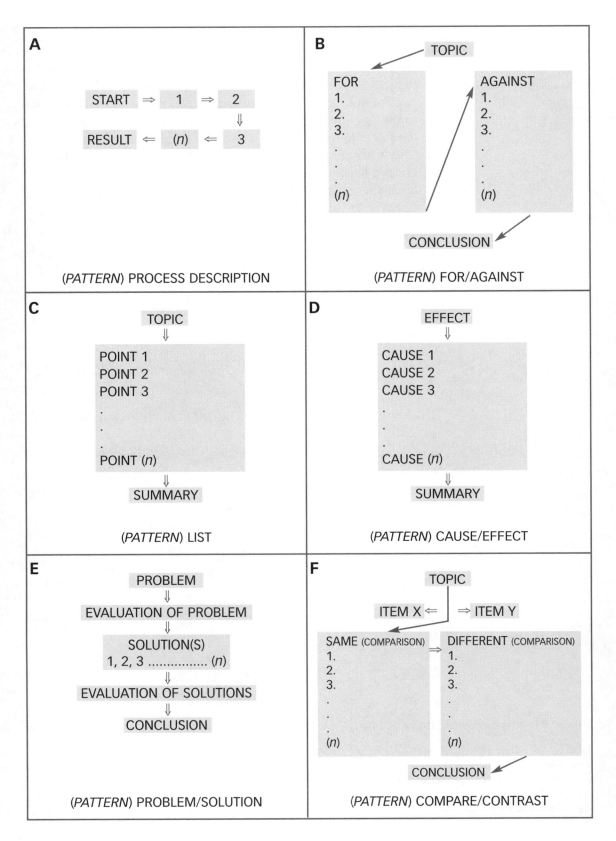

A

START ⇒ 1 ⇒ 2
⇓
RESULT ⇐ (*n*) ⇐ 3

(*PATTERN*) PROCESS DESCRIPTION

B

TOPIC

FOR
1.
2.
3.
.
.
.
(*n*)

AGAINST
1.
2.
3.
.
.
.
(*n*)

CONCLUSION

(*PATTERN*) FOR/AGAINST

C

TOPIC
⇓

POINT 1
POINT 2
POINT 3
.
.
.
POINT (*n*)

⇓
SUMMARY

(*PATTERN*) LIST

D

EFFECT
⇓

CAUSE 1
CAUSE 2
CAUSE 3
.
.
.
CAUSE (*n*)

⇓
SUMMARY

(*PATTERN*) CAUSE/EFFECT

E

PROBLEM
⇓
EVALUATION OF PROBLEM
⇓
SOLUTION(S)
1, 2, 3 .... (*n*)
⇓
EVALUATION OF SOLUTIONS
⇓
CONCLUSION

(*PATTERN*) PROBLEM/SOLUTION

F

TOPIC

ITEM X ⇐ ⇒ ITEM Y

SAME (COMPARISON)
1.
2.
3.
.
.
.
(*n*)

⇒

DIFFERENT (COMPARISON)
1.
2.
3.
.
.
.
(*n*)

CONCLUSION

(*PATTERN*) COMPARE/CONTRAST

TASK 2 Process description

1 Look at Figure 4.2 (Process description: How a Compact Disc Hi-Fi Audio System works). Put a tick beside any of the steps that you think you understand and a question mark beside those you are not sure of. (You can discuss this if you wish.) Then turn to the Key and study the passage to make sure you understand the stages in the process.

2 Check your understanding of Figure 4.2, if possible without looking back to the Key.

3 Finally write an account of this process, making the different stages in the process as clear as you can.

Vocabulary guide: Process description

Make sure you understand the following words and phrases printed in italics. They may be useful to you.

First of all	*This (just) means that …*
if this happens	*when … then*
this does not mean that …	*Finally*
The result is	*The first (second …)stage*
The reason for this is	*This stage is necessary because …*
Hence, …	

Here are some other adverbials of time that might be useful to you.

before	*previously*	*earlier*
at the same time	*simultaneously*	*concurrently*
next	*subsequently*	*after that*

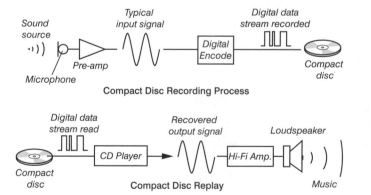

Figure 4.2 Process description: How a Compact Disc Hi-Fi Audio System works (only one channel shown)

[Source: Jim Lesurf (2003) *The Scots Guide to Electronics*. St. Andrews University, Scotland, UK
The easiest way to find this site is through:
www.IPL.org→ subject collections→ science and technology→ electronics→ The Scots Guide to Electronics]

Frame 2: Compare and contrast

When we *compare* things we look for ways in which they are the same or similar; when we *contrast* things we look for ways in which they are dissimilar or different. There are basically two ways in which we can write assignments that involve comparison and/or contrast. One way is to write down all the main points about the subjects to be compared/contrasted, then to take all the main points about the other subject as you saw in Figure 4.1 **F** (shown below).

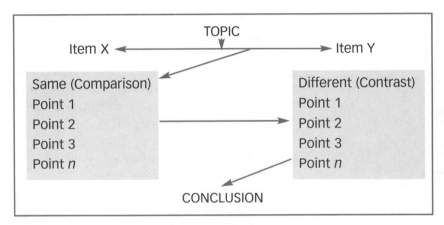

The other way is to take each point in turn and contrast them immediately, as shown below.

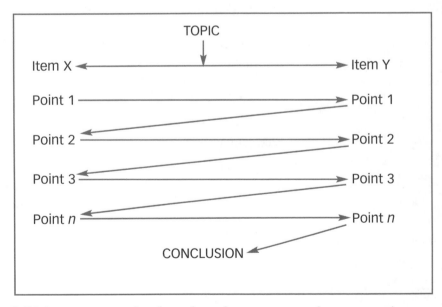

Whichever you use, be clear about how you are going to organise your assignment before you start writing it out.

TASK 3 Comparing and contrasting

1 The human mind is sometimes thought of as a very advanced
computer. Using the Vocabulary guide on p. 97 to help you,
discuss/think about, then write down:
  a) *three* ways in which human minds and computers are similar
  b) *three* ways in which they are different.

When writing, try to use a different structure for each of the six
points of comparison.

2 *(Discussion/to think about)* Look at Figure 4.3 (Patterns of
recruitment of First Year Students at UK Universities). What do
these two graphs tell you about the recruitment of students to
UK universities during the period concerned? In your answer
pay special attention to comparing and contrasting (a) the
recruitment of male and female students, and (b) the
recruitment of 'home' [UK] and 'overseas' [non-UK] students
during that period.

3 *(Discussion/to think about)* Would you say that the trends shown
here are a good thing or not?

4 *(Written assignment)* Write up your answers to questions 1 and 2
as an essay of about 150 words. The title of the essay is:
'Recruitment trends in UK Universities 1981–1999 with special
reference to male/female and home/overseas students'.
Remember to make a plan of your essay before you start writing
it. Also, have a conclusion where you can express your views on
these trends.

5 *(Written assignment)* Write an essay of at least 250 words on
one of the following topics. You will probably find it useful,
before you start writing, to make a two-column list as in the
diagrams on p. 95.

Topic 1. Compare and contrast any two sports, hobbies or pastimes
that you are familiar with.

Topic 2. Discuss the positive and negative points about the career/
profession that you might like to follow and any other career/
profession that you have considered or know something about.

Topic 3. Take any two subjects that you have studied at school or
college and compare them. Say which one you prefer and why.

Vocabulary guide: comparison/contrast
Some ways of comparing/contrasting X (e.g. soccer) and Y (e.g. rugby/golf) are given below, with the vocabulary shown in italics.

| Soccer is | *the same as*
similar to
not unlike | rugby | *in that*
because | they are both team sports. |
| Soccer | *resembles*
seems like
corresponds to | rugby | *in that*
because | it is also a team sport. |

There are several points of *similarity*
resemblance
correspondence
between soccer and rugby.

Soccer makes a lot of use of full-time professional players.
Similarly,
In the same way,
rugby is also becoming much more a professional sport.

| Golf is | *different from*
dissimilar to | soccer | *in that*
because | it is much less of a team game |
| Golf | *differs from*
bears no
  resemblance to | soccer | *in that*
because | it is not a contact sport.
golf is not a contact sport. |

Soccer is a team game.
Golf,   *on the other hand,*   is usually played by individuals.
         in contrast,

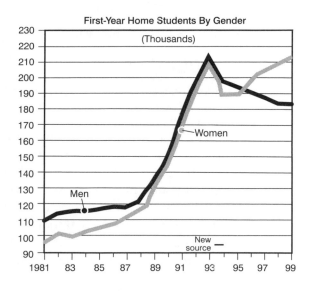

First-Year Home Students By Gender
(Thousands)

Women

Men

New source

Source: Department for Education Employment 1981–93, Higher Education Statistics Agency 1994 onwards

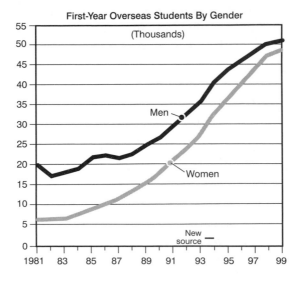

First-Year Overseas Students By Gender

(Thousands)

Men

Women

New source

Source: Department for Education Employment 1981–93, Higher Education Statistics Agency 1994 onwards

Figure 4.3 Patterns of recruitment of First Year Students at UK universities

Frame 3: Cause and effect

In discussing cause and effect we are discussing why things happen. For example, look at this sentence:

> 'John ran to the station because he wanted to be on time for the train.'

John's wish to be on time for the train is the cause; his running to the station is the effect.

For another example, look at this conversation:

> 'How did John come to break his leg?'

> 'He slipped on a banana skin.'

What is the cause and what is the effect in this example?

Simple and complex causes

A mistake often made by students is that, as in the simple examples we have been looking at, there is only one explanation (cause) for what they are trying to explain. But one effect may be due to many causes. Take a question like: 'Why was American industry located in the north of the United States rather than in the south on the eve of the civil war?' There are probably several causes for this effect. Also one cause may have several effects; or a whole series of effects, each of which cause something else to happen

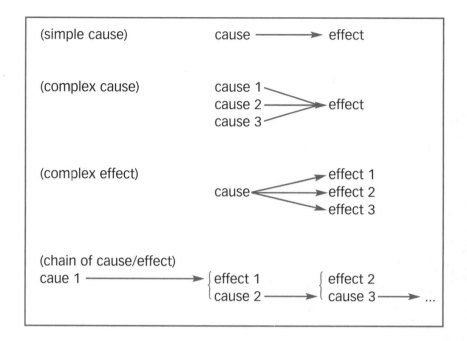

······················

TASK 4 Cause and effect

1 Answer the following questions using the Vocabulary guide given on p. 100. Try to answer each question in three different ways, using different words or phrases showing cause and effect.

   a) Why did cities in ancient times have high walls around them?

   b) Why do winds usually blow onshore (that is, from the sea) during the day and offshore at night?

   c) In many countries there is a tendency for people to leave the countryside and crowd into cities. Have you any explanation for this?

2 Using the information in Figure 4.4, explain in about 150 words the possible connection between the burning of fuels like coal and oil and the death of fish and trees.

3 Can you establish a link between the invention of the printing press and the development of democracy as a common form of government? (150 words)

Vocabulary guide: Cause and effect

As
Because   the earth is getting warmer, sea levels will get higher.
Since

	Consequently,	
	As a result,	
The earth is getting warmer.	*For this/that reason*	sea levels will get higher
	This explains why	
	So	
	The effect of this is	that sea levels will get higher.
	One result	to raise sea levels.

Resulting from
Owing to   global warming, sea levels will get higher.
Due to

The   *cause of*   higher sea levels is global warming.
One   *reason for*

Global warming is the   *cause of* higher sea levels.
                               reason for

If   the earth gets warmer, (*then*) sea levels will rise.

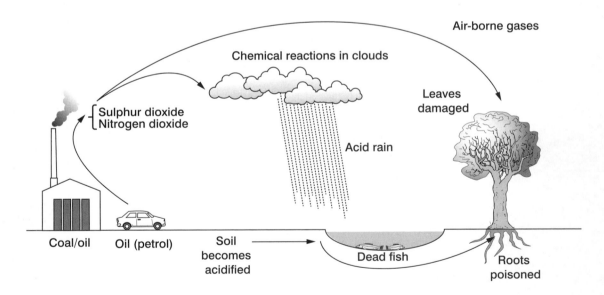

Figure 4.4 An example of how industry can damage the environment

Frame 4: For and against

In this type of assignment you are expected to take up a position either for or against something. The following is an example, where the frame is shown in *italics*.

> *Do you agree* that nuclear fuel should continue to be used as a source of energy?

Step 1. Jot down preliminary ideas.

Step 2. Research (read sources).

Step 3. Decide on your view: FOR or AGAINST.

Now you are ready to structure your assignment.

Step 4. List the arguments that support your view.

Step 5. List the counter-arguments that can be brought against your view.

Step 6. Taking each counter-argument in turn, think how you can refute (argue against) it.

Step 7. Finish by summing up.

As an alternative to Step 5, you could state all the counter-arguments one after the other, and then in a separate section take each of them in turn and refute them.

So your assignment could follow either the structure on the left or the one on the right of the diagram below.

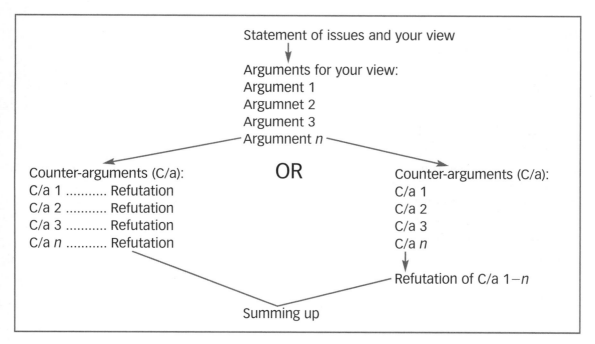

Statement of issues and your view

Arguments for your view:
Argument 1
Argumnet 2
Argument 3
Argumnent *n*

OR

Counter-arguments (C/a):
C/a 1 .... Refutation
C/a 2 .... Refutation
C/a 3 .... Refutation
C/a *n* .... Refutation

Counter-arguments (C/a):
C/a 1
C/a 2
C/a 3
C/a *n*

Refutation of C/a 1−*n*

Summing up

TASK 5 For and against

1 It has been suggested that all formal University examinations should be abolished, to be replaced by a system of continuous assessment by assignment. How far would you be prepared to support such a proposal?

　　If you are working in a group, do questions a) to d); if you are working as an individual, do questions a), e)and f).

a) Analyse this question in terms of Frame and Topic.

b) Divide into two teams, one to think up reasons for supporting this proposal, the other reasons for opposing it.

c) Note each others' arguments and try to think up counter-arguments.

d) Now what's your view?

e) Think up arguments FOR, then arguments AGAINST, then counter-arguments both FOR and AGAINST.

f) Now decide on your view.

2 Write an essay of at least 250 words responding to the assignment given in question 1, stating your own position.

Vocabulary guide: For and Against

STATING ONE'S POSITION

Personal (P)

I would like to	*agree with*	the	*proposition*	that cigarette advertising should be made illegal.
I cannot	*support*		*idea*	
			suggestion	
			view	

Impersonal (I)

The	*argument*	that cigarette advertising should be banned is	*convincing*	for the
	view		*unconvincing*	following
	proposition		*unacceptable*	reasons.
	idea			

PRESENTING EVIDENCE

Evidence which	*supports*	*this view is as follows.*
	backs up	
	confirms	
	disproves	
	refutes	
	undermines	

Firstly, …
Secondly, …
Thirdly, …
Finally, …

The first (second … final) point	(P) I'd like to make	is that …
	(I) to be made	
	that can be made	

COUNTER-ARGUMENTS
On the other hand,   *it (also) could be argued that …*
As against this,
However,

Let us take each of these	*points*	*in turn.*
	arguments	
	views	
	issues	

In response to the first (second … final)	*point,*	*it could be argued that …*
	argument	*the point could be made that*
	view	

Frame 5: Problem/solution

In this kind of assignment, a problem is described and you are asked to propose a solution to it. Usually, there will be more than one possible solution, and you will be expected to consider all noteworthy solutions, and evaluate them. This may lead you to select one or two preferred solutions unless, of course, you decide there is no viable solution. You could also be asked to look at a problem in the past and describe and evaluate the attempts to solve it.

The following is an example, where the frame is shown in *italics*.

Traffic in major cities is becoming increasingly congested. *What ideas have been proposed for solving this problem? Which ideas would you recommend for cities that have yet to overcome traffic congestion?*

This frame could therefore lead you to use the following type of structure.

Problem
⇓
Solution 1
Solution 2......
Solution *n*
⇓
Evaluation Solutions 1 ..... *(n)*
⇓
Conclusion (Preferred solution)

TASK 6 Problem/solution

1 *(Group work/To think about)* See what solutions you can brainstorm to the traffic congestion problem. You may find it useful to categorise the solutions you have come up with, such as solutions requiring different forms of public transport or solutions that reduce the number of cars in cities.

2 *(Group work/To think about)* Evaluate the different solutions you have come up with, thinking about their advantages and disadvantages. Decide on your preferred solutions with respect to any town or city that you know that suffers from traffic congestion.

3 Write an essay of at least 250 words on this topic.

With respect to any town or city that you know that suffers from traffic congestion, describe some possible solutions for the congestion. What solution(s) do you think would be most appropriate for the town/city you are concerned with?

Useful assignment techniques

So far we have been looking at *frames* which structure assignments so that they can satisfy the rubrics for the assignments. Within each assignment there are also various *techniques* that we can use to improve the quality of our response to the assignment task. The first of these is the use of *definitions*.

Using definitions and examples
When writing it is often useful to define key terms in order to prevent confusion or misunderstanding. There are various ways in which terms can be defined.

Pattern 1:   *X*   *is/means*   *Y.*
  Example:
  Psychology   is   the scientific study of the mind and behaviour.

Pattern 2:   X   is a kind of Y   which   is used for Z.
                                                    has the quality Z.

  Example:
  Name   *Category*   *Use/quality*
  An axe   is a kind of tool   (that is)   used for cutting wood.
  A bungalow   is a type of house   with only one storey.

Categories can be broad or narrow. So a tiger could be categorised as 'an animal', or more narrowly as 'a mammal', or more narrowly still as 'a member of the cat family'.

Pattern 3. It is also possible to define something by giving examples of it.

Example:

Chairs, tables, sofas, wardrobes – these are all examples of what we mean by furniture.

The trouble with this kind of definition is that it is rather loose and may not be precise enough. It also possible of course to add an example to a Pattern 1 or Pattern 2 definition to make it clearer.

Generally, you can often make your argument clearer by giving an example. But notice that you cannot prove anything by giving examples; there may be counter-examples that you have ignored or overlooked.

TASK 7 Definition

1 *(Individual/Group)* Define the following using an appropriate pattern. If you are working in a group, compare your definitions.

spade	sculptor	spear	surgeon	geology
hammer	kitchen	snake	novel	helicopter

2 *(To think about)* 'Sports by definition always involve teams.' Can you think of examples to support this statement? Can you think of any counter-examples?

3 *(Individual/Group)* Choose one of the following two topics and then write at least 150 words on the topic. Which words will have to be carefully defined?

- Democracy is the most effective method of government.
- Nationalism is the enemy of peace, and it should therefore be discouraged.

Vocabulary guide: Definition and examples

By democracy,	*we mean …*
By democracy	*is meant …*
Democracy	*is generally understood to mean/refer to …*
Democracy	is a (*kind/type/variety/form of*) government in which … that …

A (true) democrat *is a person who …*

The (main) *distinguishing/distinctive features of* democracy are …

In its true/real sense, nationalism *means …*

By nationalism,	*I do not mean …*
Nationalism	*is not to be confused with …*

Nationalism	*is to*	be	*distinguished from …*
	must		

For example, …
For instance, …
By way of an example, let's take a sport like golf.
A good example of a team sport would be football.

Evidence, implication and inference

Whatever kind of assignment you write, you will want to support your argument with evidence. Unless you are collecting your own data, most of this evidence will come from your sources.

Note: data can be treated either as a plural noun (*these data*) or as an uncountable noun (*this data*).

When you are quoting from a source sometimes the meaning is straightforward. At other times you may have to think about what the statement implies (suggests), as well as its obvious meaning. For example, if I say 'Every book I have read on this topic supports my point of view' this *implies*, and the reader is entitled to *infer* (assume), that I have read a number of books on the topic. If I have read only one book on the topic, then this is a misleading statement.

Let us take another example. The famous writer and humorist, Mark Twain, once said:

> 'It is very easy to give up smoking. I've done it dozens of times.'

Here, of course, what is implied is the opposite of what it seems to say. Mark Twain is telling us that he actually finds it very difficult to give up smoking.

Do not confuse *imply* and *infer*. See how they are used:

The writer (Mark Twain) *implies* that it is actually very difficult to stop smoking.

The reader *infers*

TASK 8 Evidence, implication and inference

1 *(To think about)* What are the qualities that you think are important in a good lecture? Make a list of them in order of importance.

2 Now look at the tables in Figure 4.5.

   a) How do you think these data were obtained?

   b) What are the three most important qualities of a good lecture according to Arts students in: (i) Cambridge; (ii) Leeds; (iii) Southampton?

   c) What are the three most important qualities of a good lecture according to Science students in: (i) Cambridge; (ii) Leeds; (iii) Southampton; (iv) Northampton?

   d) How reliable is this evidence about university students in general, in your opinion? (For example, are the results consistent across all the universities listed? What might account for the differences? Do you think the results might be different in other countries?)

3 What might you infer from these data about the different preferences of Arts and Science students with reference to lectures?

4 Using the data from Figure 4.5, and also your own data from your answer to question 1, write about 250 words on one of these topics:
- What students expect from a good lecturer
- What students expect from a good teacher.

Vocabulary guide: Evidence, implication and inference

This evidence	*shows us*	*that …*		
		demonstrates		
		proves		

| *It is* | *clear* | *from this evidence that …* | | |
| | *obvious* | | | |

On the basis of	*this evidence*	*we may*	*conclude*	*that …*
	these data		*infer*	
	this data			
		it seems	*likely*	*that …*
			possible	
			probable	

The writer (clearly) implies that …

We can infer from the evidence given here that …

| *One* | *implication of this evidence is that …* |
| *The* | |

| *One* | *inference we can make from this evidence is that …* |
| *The* | |

The writer shows us that Arts and Science students responded differently *and therefore, by implication,* that Arts and Science students have different requirements when they listen to lectures.

Arts students

Proportion of students mentioning –	Cambridge	Leeds	Southampton
Delivery	57%	50%	36%
Notes	11%	8%	8%
Clarity	38%	45%	41%
Interest	49%	38%	41%
Originality	33%	32%	51%
Guidance	14%	30%	31%
Comprehensibility	6%	15%	21%
Grasp of subject	6%	13%	3%
Illustration	2%	5%	14%
Openness to questioning	1%	10%	13%
Factual coverage	1%	–	3%
Other	8%	2%	3%
Number of students	63	40	39

Science students

Proportion of students mentioning –	Cambridge	Leeds	Southampton	Northampton
Delivery	53%	37%	30%	22%
Notes	43%	37%	56%	20%
Clarity	59%	26%	32%	37%
Interest	37%	28%	23%	23%
Originality	2%	4%	2%	2%
Guidance	18%	24%	16%	22%
Comprehensibility	20%	26%	32%	45%
Grasp of subject	12%	13%	18%	42%
Illustration	6%	13%	14%	5%
Openness to questioning	–	13%	7%	5%
Factual coverage	4%	7%	5%	8%
Other	6%	4%	4%	8%
Number of students	49	46	57	92

[Source: Peter Marris (1964) *The Experience of Higher Education* Hove, East Sussex: Routledge and Kegan Paul]

Figure 4.5 Table of students' assessment of a good lecturer

Drafting and re-drafting

When you are writing an answer in an exam you will probably have time to write your answer only once, perhaps with minor corrections. However, when writing an assignment that is not timed, you should be able to write more than one draft. Re-drafting is especially painless if you use a word processor (computer) for your writing, and it can greatly enhance the quality of your written work.

Re-drafting usually takes place in two stages:

Stage 1. Evaluating overall impact. At this stage you are concerned with 'the big picture' – the overall impact of your assignment. Is the argument clear and will it impress the reader?

Stage 2. Proofreading. Here you are concerned with more surface matters like points of style, spelling, punctuation and minor inaccuracies.

TASK 9 Evaluating overall impact

A student has been asked to write an essay of not more than 450 words on this topic:

Proposal for a graduate tax

In country X all state education, including higher education, is free to suitably qualified students. The government is now proposing to introduce a 'graduate tax' whereby all graduate students will have to repay the full cost of their higher education over a period of 10 years. What do you think of this proposal?

The student's first draft follows. Read it and then do Task 9.

I don't see why people should pay for higher education. After all, state primary and secondary education are free, why not state higher education? Anyway, it is in the country's interest to have all its citizens educated to the best of their ability. An educated workforce is the real wealth of a country. Everybody benefits from it, not just the ones who have been educated. If graduates have to repay the full cost of their fees, many clever people will be discouraged from going into higher education, and the whole country will suffer. Also, a university education is more than just a preparation for work. It is every citizen's human right to be freely educated according to their ability and their interests.

   Some people argue that graduates earn more than people who do not have degrees, and so they can afford to pay the extra graduate tax. But this is not fair. Not all the jobs that graduates do are well paid. Also there are many people who do not go to university, but go straight into a trade or into business and some of these people can end up being quite wealthy. Why should only the graduates be penalised? Also, the graduates have already been 'taxed' in a sense, because for many years they have not been able to earn the salaries they would have earned if they had gone straight into business after school.

Another argument for a graduate tax is that students will take their studies more seriously if they know they will eventually have to pay for them. But this argument is irrelevant. If students don't take their studies seriously, they will fail and never graduate, and so they won't pay the tax anyway.

(288 words)

1 *(To think about)* Think back to the various frameworks (ways of organising assignments) that you have been shown in this unit. Which framework is closest to the one this writer has used? In what way does this essay differ from the 'ideal' framework?
2 *(To think about)* What would you say are the strengths and weaknesses of this essay, in terms of its general impact? How could it be improved?

(At the end of your period of thought or discussion, see the Key for the tutor's comments on this first draft. Note that tutors don't usually comment on first drafts of short essays – that is why you have to learn to do it for yourself!)

Overall impact: cohesion and signposting
Many first drafts suffer from not being coherent enough and from being inadequately signposted.

Your essay will have much greater impact if you:
- signpost the structure in a helpful way
- make it clear to the reader how the argument coheres ('hangs together').

Here are some ways of achieving this.

Introduction. Have an introduction in which you clearly state what the issue is (as you understand it), what your argument is and how you are going to structure it.

Conclusion. Have a conclusion in which you clearly summarise the most important parts of your argument.

Headings and sub-headings. In longer assignments (over 2,000 words) use headings and sub-headings to break up the text and make your structure clear.

Cohesive markers. These are words and phrases which you can use to show how the various parts of your argument fit together, for example *firstly, secondly, on the other hand.* (See the Vocabulary guide below.)

Abstract. In longer assignments it may be useful to provide an abstract at the beginning that summarises the whole assignment.

TASK 10 Improving overall impact

Make a second draft of the essay in Task 9. You can keep the basic content the same or similar, but concentrate on improving the overall impact.

Vocabulary guide: cohesion and signposting.
(Introduction)

| *In this* | *essay* | *I will* | *argue* | *against* | X. |
| | *assignment* | *intend to* | | *for* | |

(Personal)
I will begin by …
Then I will …
Finally I will …
(Impersonal)

First,	*it will be argued that*
Then,	
Finally,	

(Main section)

First, let me say why	*I reject this idea.*		
	I find this	*proposal*	*unacceptable.*
		suggestion	
		idea	
		argument	

My	*second*	*argument*	*is …*
	third	*point*	
	final	*objection*	

Now let us look at some of the	*arguments* *points*	*that have been*	*advanced to* *put forward*	*justify* *defend*	*this*	*proposal.* *position.*

(Conclusion)
To sum up, …
In conclusion, …

I have	*rejected* *accepted*	*this*	*proposal for* *idea*	*two* *three* (n)	*main* *key*	*reasons.*

In this	*paper,* *assignment* *essay*	*it has been*	*argued* *suggested*	*that …*

Proofreading

This is the second and final stage of re-drafting.

Study the proofreading hints given below then do Task 11.

At this stage, you are still very much concerned with making sure that your meaning is clear, but you are especially interested in details, such as:

- *spelling* – especially the spelling of authors' names
- *punctuation*
- *pages* numbered and their correct order
- whether the *style* is appropriate. Is it too personal for the type of assignment you are writing? Should it be more impersonal?
- whether the *grammar* is correct.

If you are using a computer, you will find the spell-check and grammar-check invaluable, but they may not be of much help with proper names.

References are a frequent source of error. Note the difference between a *bibliography* (a list of books etc. on the topic, whether you have actually made reference to them or not) and a *list of references*, which is a list of all the sources you have used for your assignment.

Make sure:
- all sources referred to in the text are listed in the list of references
- references are
  - in the correct alphabetical order
  - displayed in the appropriate style
  - complete (in that they contain all the required source information).

The importance of surnames

Remember that it is an author's surname (family name) that is most important for alphabetical ordering. The surname is usually the name that comes last. For example in:

Judith Bell

the order of the names tells us that the writer's surname is Bell. Sometimes (for example in a list of references) the order of the names is reversed, so that the surname is printed first. This unusual order is indicated by a COMMA after the surname. So if you see someone's name written like this:

Bell, Judith

the presence of the comma tells you that Bell is this writer's surname, not her first name.

Basic rules for alphabetical order of authors are:

Go through the author's surname letter by letter until you find the letter which comes earlier in the alphabet. So, as BRA*N* comes before BRA*U*, then:

Brand, W.G.
Braun, A.C.
Breslin, A.A.

are in the correct order.

Remember, though, that as far as surnames are concerned, 'nothing comes before something', so that these names are in the correct order:

Brown, J.A.
Browning, A.R.
Browning, M.J.

Although names beginning with Mac/Mc/M' are all pronounced as if they were Mac, they are usually listed in strict letter-by-letter alphabetical order. The apostrophe in M' is ignored for listing purposes. These names are in the correct order:

MacArthur, L.
MacNeil, R.B.
McAllister, C.F.
M'Carthy, T.S.

Sources by the same author are listed by date of publication, for example:

Kim, L.S. (1991)
Kim, L.S. (1994)

Sources by the same author published in the same year listed by the first letter of the title, ignoring *A* and *The*. The order of the entries is shown by the lower-case letters a, b, c and so on, after the date.

Kaufman, J.R. (1990a) *Control of...*
Kaufman, J.R. (1990b) *Roles of...*

[Guidelines and some of the examples have been taken from the *Publication Manual of the American Psychological Assocation 4th Edn* (1994), which can be referred to for more detailed guidelines.]

TASK 11 Proofreading a list of references

1 You will see below a list of references taken from an academic source. Study the list and, either on your own or in a group, try to work out what style rules the writer followed when he was making up this list of references. (For example, one rule that he followed is that all the names are in strict alphabetical order.) You should find at least ten 'style rules'. When you have finished, check your list against the Key.

References

Anderson, J.R. (2000). *Cognitive Psychology and its Implications* (5th ed.). New York: Worth Publishers.

Bailey, K.M. (1993). 'The use of diary studies in teacher education programs.' in J.C. Richards and D. Nunan (Eds.) *Second Language Teacher Education*. Cambridge: Cambridge University Press.

Dennet, D. (1993). *Consciousness Explained*. London: Penguin Books.

Goleman, D. (1996). *Emotional Intelligence*. London: Bloomsbury.

Greenfield, S. (2000). *The Private Life of the Brain*. London: Penguin Books.

Hunt, M. (1984). *The Universe Within: A new science explores the human mind*. London: Corgi Books.

Lodge, D. (2001). *Thinks…* London: Secker and Warburg.

Lodge, D. (2002). *Conciousness and the Novel* London: Secker and Warburg.

Richards, J.C. (1998) (Ed.). *Teaching in Action: Case studies from second language classrooms*. Alexandria, Virginia: TESOL Inc.

---

2 Below is a list of references submitted by a student who has written an assignment on some aspect of professionalism. The student has made *five* serious mistakes. Can you spot what they are?

Coady, M. and Bloch, S. (Eds.) (1996). <u>Codes of Ethics and the Professions</u>. Victoria, Australia: Melbourne University Press.

Krause, E.A. (1996). <u>Death of the Guilds: Professions, states and the advance of capitalism, 1930 to the present</u>. New Haven, Connecticut/London: Yale University Press.

Saks, M. (1995). <u>Professions and the Public Interest: Medical power, altruism and alternative medicine.</u> London: Routledge.

Malin, N. (Ed.) (2000). <u>Professionalism, Boundaries and the Workplace.</u> Routledge.

Neal, M. and Morgan, J. (2000). The professionalization of everyone? A comparative study of the development of the professions in the United Kingdom and Germany. <u>European Sociological Review.</u>

Fisher, J., Gunz, S. and McCutcheon, J. (2001). Public/private interest and the enforcement of a code of professional conduct. <u>Journal of Business Ethics</u>, 31/3: 191–208.

Witz, A. <u>Professions and Patriarchy</u>. London: Routledge.

TASK 12 **Drafting and re-drafting an assignment**

Note: you may find the checklist that follows useful for this and other assignment tasks.

In this Task, you are asked to complete steps 1 to 5 below, for an assignment you select from the bulleted list that follows (or another of your own choosing).

1 Write a first draft of an assignment.
2 Check the first draft for overall impact. Note: if you are working in a group, exchange drafts and check each other's work.
3 Make changes as appropriate in your first draft.
4 Proofread your second draft carefully. Note: as before, if you are working in a group, exchange drafts and check each other's work.
5 Submit your final draft for evaluation.

Some suggested assignment tasks are given below, but you may prefer to work on a topic of your own choosing.

- It has been proposed that the use of nuclear energy for generating energy should be banned. What are your views?
- 'All international sports and athletics should be run on a strictly amateur basis.' Discuss.
- In many countries the birth rate has fallen so low that the population is actually shrinking. What do you think are the reasons for this trend? What, if anything, should governments be doing about it?
- Compare and contrast the issue of global warming as it affects rich and poor nations. What conclusions do you draw from your comparison?
- What do you understand by the term genetic modification? Is it a good thing?

(**Note:** More detailed approaches to academic writing will be found in Liz Hamp-Lyons and Ben Heasley (2004) *Study Writing*, Cambridge: Cambridge University Press.)

CHECKLIST for assignments

Pre-writing stage

- What is the weighting of this assignment in your course assessment?
- Do you know and understand the criteria for marking the assignment?
- Do you understand the assignment title?
- Can you divide it into frame and topic?
- What are the keywords in the topic?
- What is the frame? Can you think of an appropriate organisation framework?
- Do you already have some ideas of your own on this topic? If so, what are they?
- Will you have to do any basic research?
- If so, what sources of data and information are available to you?

Content

- Is your content sufficiently comprehensive? (For example, in a discussion, have you considered ALL the arguments for and against?)
- Have you produced evidence to support your argument?
- Have you been sufficiently self-critical? (For example, have you thought of contrary arguments, contrary evidence?)
- Have you been able to rebut (refute) contrary arguments/evidence?
- (Plagiarism.) If you have used someone else's words or ideas, has this been duly acknowledged? (In other words, have you made it clear what your source is, and where that source can be found?)
- Where your sources are in conflict, have you made your own position clear?
- Is there any content that is irrelevant to your argument?
- Is there any unnecessary repetition?

Organisation and presentation

- If you have used an abstract have you made your main conclusions clear?
- Have you begun with a helpful overview?
- Is your argument clearly signposted with appropriate use of headings/sub-headings and discourse markers?
- Have you used diagrams etc. where they would clarify your argument?
- Have you ended with a helpful summary or conclusion?

Re-drafting/proofreading

- Have you carefully read the assignment through, assessing its overall impact?
- Have you checked for errors in grammar, spelling (NB proper names) and punctuation?
- Have you checked that all your sources are in your List of References?
- Have you carefully checked your Bibliography/List of References for errors, omissions and/or inaccuracies?

Note: This checklist may be freely photocopied.

UNIT 5 Learning through discussions

This unit aims to help you to:

1. develop proficiency practice in extended oral interaction, that is in speaking for longer periods as in discussions or presentations
2. develop strategies for effective participation in discussion
3. develop effective oral presentation skills.

The unit will progress in three stages, corresponding to the three aims just listed.

Stage 1: Oral interaction

TASK 1 **Pair work: Questions and answers on personal topics**
In pairs, think of *ten* topics of personal interest that both of you can talk about. For example:

> Your family
> Favourite sports/hobbies/pastimes
> Favourite books/films/TV shows
> School-related topics

When you have agreed on ten topics, divide them at random between the two of you. Each of you will then choose one of the five topics allocated to your partner and ask him or her at least six questions about it. In order to get longer answers, try to ask 'Wh-' questions rather than 'yes/no' questions. For example, instead of 'Did you study French at school?' ask 'What subjects did you study at school?' You can also ask follow-up questions to the answer.

When you have each discussed one topic, you can then go on to the next pair of topics, and so on.

TASK 2 **Pair work: 'Long turns' on personal topics**
One of the main things you will need to learn in higher education is how to explain your ideas and opinions; and to discuss the ideas and opinions of your fellow students. This kind of more extended interaction with others involves more extended turns of interaction – sometimes language teachers call these 'long turns'.

The purpose of the next task is to allow you the chance of speaking and listening at slightly greater length (one or two minutes), but still about personal matters. You will be given a minute to prepare your talk.

Below you will find two topics – **A** and **B** – each with three subtopics. For topic **A**, decide who will be the 'speaker' and who the 'listener'. If you are the speaker study the first topic carefully, underlining any keywords. Then prepare your answer. You can make notes but **remember that you will only have a minute to prepare your talk**.

While the speaker is doing this, the listener should try to think of at least *two* follow-up questions that will probably be relevant. While the speaker is speaking it is important to give them **your full attention**. At the end of the talk you should ask one or two follow-up questions, which may be the ones you prepared, or others that occurred to you while you were listening. (You can make a note while you are listening if a question occurs to you.)

For topic **B**, the roles are reversed.

Topic **A**
Describe a journey that you have taken or a place that you have visited that you found interesting or enjoyable.

- What age were you?
- Who, if anyone, was with you?
- What was it that made the experience interesting or enjoyable?

Topic **B**
Describe a public occasion (for example a festival/party/ceremony) that was particularly memorable for you.

- When (how long ago) did it take place?
- What was the nature of the occasion?
- Why did it make such an impression on you?

TASK 3 **Pair work: 'Long turns' on more academic topics**
Prepare the following topics in the same way as for Task 2.

Topic **A**
It has been argued that examinations are unfair and an inappropriate form of assessment in higher education, and that regular course assessment by assignments would be better. What are your views?

- Think of examinations you have taken. Were they fair and appropriate?
- Do you think that examinations are more appropriate for some subjects or areas of study than others?
- What is the best way of assessing students' work?

Topic **B**

Some students choose to (or perhaps have to) work at part-time unskilled jobs while they are attending college or university. What are your views?

- Do you think that doing such work should be avoided if you can afford it?
- What are the advantages/disadvantages of students doing part-time unskilled work?
- If a student decided to do some part-time work, what would be the best kind of work for him or her to do?

Stage 2: Effective participation in discussion

The rationale for discussions

Perhaps we should start by thinking about why we might take part in an academic discussion, as opposed to, say, reading books or attending lectures.

TASK 4 **Reasons for participating in academic discussions**

Listed below are ten reasons for taking part in an academic discussion session. I'd like you to rate each reason on a scale of 1 to 5 stars. So if you think one of the statements is a very important reason for taking part in academic discussions give it 5*; if it is of only average importance give it 3*, and if it is not a good reason at all then give it 1*, and so on. Then compare your rating with those of others in your group.

Reason	Rating
1 It helps students to understand the subject more deeply	
2 It is a chance to get to know other students better	
3 It improves students' ability to think	
4 It is more relaxing than listening to a lecture	
5 It helps to solve particular problems	
6 It gives you a chance to share ideas and insights with other students	
7 You don't have to take notes	
8 It gives you a chance to practise your English	
9 It gives you more confidence in speaking	
10 It can change your ideas	

Can you think of any other reasons not listed here?

The conduct of a discussion

A discussion is a group activity. The usefulness of a discussion depends on many things, but two of the most important are:

- how the individual members of the group (*the participants*) behave
- how the group as a whole behaves.

TASK 5 Behaviour: individual participants

This task is concerned with the behaviour of individual participants. Participants' attitudes may be positive or negative. By positive attitudes we mean ways of behaving that are helpful to the discussion. Negative attitudes, on the other hand, are unhelpful. Listed below are twenty ways of behaving in a discussion. Opposite each statement, circle either P (for positive) or N (for negative). Circle query (?) if you are not sure. Then compare notes with the other members of the group. Hopefully you will be largely in agreement!

The student:			
1 has previously thought about the topic	P	N	?
2 is willing to listen to others	P	N	?
3 never takes anything seriously	P	N	?
4 is willing to change his/her opinion	P	N	?
5 makes long speeches	P	N	?
6 is not afraid to say what he/she truly believes	P	N	?
7 will not give others a chance to speak	P	N	?
8 will talk only to the tutor, ignoring other participants	P	N	?
9 encourages other participants to speak	P	N	?
10 makes sarcastic remarks	P	N	?
11 is tolerant of others' point of view	P	N	?
12 makes his/her points concisely (briefly)	P	N	?
13 becomes angry or upset easily	P	N	?
14 will support good ideas from other participants	P	N	?
15 interrupts others before they have a chance to finish	P	N	?
16 pretends to agree with the rest of the group though he/she really does not	P	N	?
17 can relieve a tense or emotional situation with humour	P	N	?
18 shows how his/her own comments build on points that previous speakers have made	P	N	?
19 holds whispered conversations with his/her neighbour	P	N	?
20 thinks that time spent on discussion is time wasted	P	N	?

Can you think of any other ways in which individual participants can contribute to the success of a discussion?

········
······················
········

TASK 6 Behaviour: group

This task is concerned with how the group as a whole behaves. Below, there is a list of ten factors that might affect the usefulness of a discussion. Working either individually or as a group, take each factor in turn and decide whether it is positive (P), negative (N), or you are not sure (?).

In the discussion:			
1 everyone talks at the same time	P	N	?
2 the group has clearly defined aims (it knows exactly what it is supposed to be achieving)	P	N	?
3 there is a timetable for different stages of the discussion	P	N	?
4 some participants just take notes all the time, without saying anything	P	N	?
5 there is some time at the end for summing up what has been agreed or decided	P	N	?
6 no one takes any notes	P	N	?
7 everyone contributes by saying something	P	N	?
8 at the end, each student is aware of the views of the other members of the group	P	N	?
9 all participants leave with the same ideas and opinions they came in with	P	N	?
10 most of the opinions expressed are supported by evidence of some kind	P	N	?

Think of discussions that you have taken part in. How usual is it for such discussions to be successful, in your opinion? What in your opinion is the factor that most often undermines the success of a discussion?

Can you think of any practical steps that could be taken to ensure the success of discussions?

Defining terms and using evidence
Defining terms

Do you agree with this statement: 'Women are better drivers than men'? You may say that you cannot answer until you know what is meant by the phrase *better drivers*. This phrase could perhaps mean:

- safer drivers
- faster drivers
- more courteous drivers
- more cautious drivers
- drivers more interested in the machines
- some combination of the above.

Perhaps someone who agrees with this opinion means all of these things, or some of them, or something else entirely. It is very difficult to have a useful discussion if everyone is actually talking about different things. Before a discussion, or perhaps during a discussion it may be necessary for participants to *define their terms*.

It may also be necessary to specify what certain key terms refer to (that is, to specify *the terms of reference*). For example, when we are referring to men/women drivers, are we thinking of drivers in a certain country or do we mean drivers everywhere?

Identifying terms that may have to be defined

TASK 7

1 Look at the following statements of opinion. Underline any terms (words or phrases) that you think might have to be defined before a meaningful discussion can take place.
   a) Democracy is definitely the best way of running a country.
   b) Scientists should be allowed to perform any kind of experiment they like: otherwise progress will come to a halt.
   c) In this day and age, people cannot consider themselves truly educated unless they have studied a scientific subject in some depth.
   d) The urban (city-based) way of life is obviously an unnatural way of life, and that is another reason why people should be discouraged from moving into the towns.
   e) I think that everyone will agree that the first duty of a government is to ensure that everyone gets a fair wage.
   f) The highest wages ought to be paid to those who actually do the work – in other words the members of the working class.
2 Compare your underlined terms with others in your group. Pick any term that everyone agrees requires to be defined and individually write down your definition of that term. Compare your definition with the others. See if you can agree on a definition that is acceptable to everyone (or at least to the majority!).

Vocabulary guide

To me,	*the term X is ambiguous/vague/confusing*
I find	

I think	*X could have several possible*	*meanings*
In my opinion,		*interpretations*

One possible meaning	*of X is …*
interpretation	

I	*would take X to mean …*
	interpret X in this way: …
	think X means …

Another way of defining/interpreting X would be …

Using evidence

Usually a person who puts forward an opinion should be able to support it with evidence. The most convincing kind of evidence is usually evidence that other people can check or verify.

TASK 8 Establishing potentially useful evidence

1 Let us think again about this opinion: Women are better drivers than men. Let us imagine that the group has discussed the definition of 'better drivers' and agreed that by 'better drivers' it means 'safer drivers'.

   Say how useful the following kinds of evidence would be in a discussion of this kind:
   a) one member of the group knows a woman driver who is very careless and forgetful;
   b) a comparison of the percentage of men drivers and women drivers found guilty of dangerous driving within a specific recent period;
   c) the number of claims that women drivers make on their car insurance companies as compared to men drivers.

Is there any other information you would need to know before you could accept or reject the various bits of evidence given above?

Note: The evidence in a) is based on someone's experience, sometimes called *anecdotal evidence*. The evidence in b) and c) is based on statistics (*statistical evidence*).

2 Look at the following statements of opinion. What kind of evidence would be useful for a discussion of these topics?
   a) Smoking cigarettes is bad for your health.
   b) Hanging is a deterrent to murder (that is, some murders would not be committed if murderers knew they would be hanged if caught and found guilty).
   c) When workers go on strike, the reason given for the strike is usually a wage claim of some kind. But the real reason for most strikes is boring and unpleasant working conditions.
   d) The showing of violent scenes on TV and in films involving the use of guns is the reason for the increased use of guns by criminals these days.

Stage 3: Developing effective oral presentation skills

At one time, most university teaching took the form of giving formal lectures. Nowadays, many lecturers try to involve their students more actively in the learning process. One of the ways in which this is done is by conducting seminars. What usually happens in a seminar is that one student is asked to introduce the topic. (Let's call this person 'the presenter'.) After the presenter has introduced the topic it can then be discussed by all the participants.

There are two main stages involved in presenting a paper:
- the preparation stage
- the presentation stage.

The preparation stage

The preparation stage involves five steps:
1 making sure you understand the topic
2 making sure you understand the frame (given in the rubric, that is the instructions as to what to do)
3 generating your own preliminary ideas on the topic
4 researching the topic
5 writing up the topic.

It will be clear that the processes involved in the preparation stage for an oral presentation are very similar to those involved in a written presentation. The techniques involved in preparing for a written presentation are dealt with in more detail in Units 3 and 4.

The presentation stage

TASK 9 **Individual or group**

What follows is a list of tips that have been given on making a short oral presentation on a topic for discussion. Rate each recommendation on a scale going from 5* down to 1* where 5* means 'extremely important' and 1* means 'not at all important'.

Tips for short oral presentations

1 **Time limit.** Your tutor may give you a time limit, or you may be allowed to decide for yourself. If it is the latter, let your audience know what it is and make sure that it leaves plenty of time for discussion. *Do not exceed your limit.*

Rating_____

2 **Full version of presentation.** Write out everything you have to say, including examples and so on, then rehearse it until you feel comfortable with it.

Rating_____

3 **Outline notes.** Reduce your talk to outline notes. Rehearse your talk again, this time from the outline notes. Speak from the outline notes. (But bring along the full version, just in case!)   **Rating**_____

4 **Shared outline with audience.** It will probably help your audience if you share your outline notes, or perhaps just the main headings, with them. Some ways of doing this are:

■ *OHP (overhead projector).* Make sure that what you have written can be easily read, even from the back of the room.

■ *Chalkboard/Flipchart.* Preferably written up beforehand – but see OHP comment.

■ *Handout.* Leave plenty of room between the headings for participants to make their own notes.

■ *Powerpoint (computer) presentation.* (But see OHP comment.)   **Rating**_____

5 **Eye contact.** As far as possible, look at your audience while you are speaking. While you are looking at your audience, try to sense if they are understanding you. You will never make contact with your audience if your eyes are constantly fixed on the paper in front of you.   **Rating**_____

6 **Helpful overview.** Start by very briefly reminding your audience of the topic and summarising in a sentence or two what you are going to say and/or how you are going to deal with the topic.   **Rating**_____

7 **Signposting.** Your talk should be clearly structured, and the language you use should signpost the structure (that is, make clear to the audience what the structure is: main points/examples/digressions/summary and so on).   **Rating**_____

8 **Strong ending.** Leave time for a strong ending. One way of doing this is simply to emphasise the most important point that you have made in your talk, but you may think of another good way of ending, depending on the topic. Welcome comments from the other participants.   **Rating**_____

I'm sure you have been at 'the receiving end' of oral presentations often enough. Can you think of any other useful tips for presenters?

···················
: **TASK 10** **Oral presentations and discussion**
: The final part of this unit gives you the chance to put the techniques we have been discussing into practice. There are different ways that this can be organised, and a few of them are suggested below.

Basic format. The basic format is that one participant (*the presenter*) will give a lead-in talk on a topic, which will be discussed by the other participants. The presentation and the discussion should be the subject of *feedback/evaluation* (see below).

Topic. The best thing would be for the presenter to choose a topic that she or he is interested in and knows something about. However, it is important that the topic should be one that can interest the other participants and one that they are likely to have views on. Alternatively, you can choose one of the topics listed below (under 'Possible seminar topics').

Length of presentation. This will be decided by your tutor: normally it would be take 20–30 per cent of the time available. The other participants can take notes during the presentation.

Preparation of presentation. This would normally be done by the presenter, but in a larger group it can be done by a small group of two or three people, one of whom is chosen to be the presenter. As well as using their own ideas, presenters should ideally do some basic research on the topic (see Unit 3).

Discussion. The discussion should be chaired either by the tutor or by one of the participants. If there are only a few participants, then the presenter can chair. It is often useful to summarise at the end the main points that have been raised or conclusions that have been reached.

Feedback/evaluation. This can be done either by one or two of the participants acting as observers, or by the group as a whole after the discussion. About 15 minutes should be left for the evaluation process. Feedback/evaluation checklists have been provided on pp. 129-130. It might be possible for the tutor to give preliminary feedback to the presenter(s) while the other participants are filling in feedback forms. If the facilities are available and time allows, it might be useful to record the presentation on video/audiotape so that the feedback can be illustrated using the recording. One advantage of taping is that it makes it easier to focus on the language used, as well as the content. Special attention can be given to interrupting, claiming one's turn and so forth.

Possible seminar topics (with topic area in brackets)
Below are a series of statements that you may either agree or disagree with. Prepare an introductory talk in which you explain the issues involved and in which you make your own views clear. You may find some of the advice given in Unit 4, on topics and frames in written presentations, useful here too.

Also, remember that it is possible to agree with part of the position as stated, and disagree with another part of it.

- (**The developing world**) International aid programmes are totally ineffective in relieving world poverty and should be abolished. All that happens is that money is taken from poor people in rich countries and given to rich people in poor countries.
- (**The physical world**) In order to save the environment it is necessary that activities that can damage it should be heavily taxed. Thus all air travel should be heavily taxed so that non-essential journeys (by tourists, for example) will be discouraged.
- (**Diet**) Eating meat and fish necessarily involves cruelty to other living creatures. Vegetarianism should be made compulsory.
- (**Language policy**) Promoting the use of English (or any other national language) as an international language can easily turn into a new form of colonialism (neo-colonialism). The United Nations should choose an artificial language (such as Esperanto) and promote it as the universal second language.
- (**Culture**) Cultural differences cause disharmony. Children should be taught to think internationally, rather than being drilled in their own history and culture.
- (**Equal rights**) Although they constitute about half the population, women are badly under-represented in most governments. Political parties everywhere should be compelled to ensure that at least 50 per cent of their candidates are women.
- (**Energy policy**) In view of the dangers created by global warming, the use of nuclear power has to be continued and, indeed, further developed.
- (**Sport**) Sport today is far too commercialised. In high-profile athletics competitions such as the Olympic Games we should return to the ideal of sport performed only by amateurs.

Vocabulary guide
[Presentation]
The topic of my talk today is ….
I'd like to begin by ….
My talk will be organised like this. First, …

And so we come to my first/second/third … point.
The first/second/third point I want to make is this.

For instance/For example …
Let me give you (another) example.
I'd like to sum up by repeating a point I made earlier (which is this.)

Let me (very briefly) summarise the main points I want to make.

If you have any questions I'd be pleased/happy to answer them (if I can).

[Discussion]
[Questioning/Clarification]
I'd like to ask you about (what you said   concerning …
                                        on the subject of …)

I wasn't very clear about …

May I ask a question?
Could you please explain to us again the point you made about …

[Interrupting/Turn-taking]
Can I just come in there? Please do/Yes, of course.

I'd like to pick up on something the last speaker said.

[Disagreeing]
I think that's a very good point, but I also feel/think that …

I'm afraid I can't (really/quite) agree   with that point.
                                        the point just made.

[Round-up/Summary]
Looking back on our discussion,
    it seems to me that the main points that have come up are   these.
                                                              as follows.

OK, let's try to summarise the main points that have come up (in our discussion).

> (**Note:** More detailed approaches to seminar discussions and presentation, together with audio inputs, can be found in Tony Lynch and Kenneth Anderson (2004) *Study Speaking*. Cambridge: Cambridge University Press.)

FEEDBACK/EVALUATION:

(1) PRESENTATION

1 Mention any particular strengths in the presentation.

2 a) Was an outline of the talk shared
   with the audience?   YES/NO

   b) Was it clear?   YES/NO   (WHY/WHY NOT?)

   c) Was it helpful?   YES/NO   (WHY/WHY NOT?)

3 Did the speaker maintain good eye
   contact with the participants?   YES/NO

4 a) Did the speaker give an overview
   of what the talk was going to
   be about?   YES/NO

   b) Was it helpful?   YES/NO   (WHY/WHY NOT?)

5 Was the structure/organisation of
   the talk clear?   YES/NO

6 a) Was there any time when you did
   not understand the speaker or
   lost the thread of his or
   her argument?   YES/NO

   b) If YES, what do you think caused
   the breakdown in comprehension?

7 What about the pace/speed of
   delivery?   (TOO FAST/TOO SLOW/JUST
                                     RIGHT?)

8 Was there a strong ending?   YES/NO
   (If NO, how could it have been improved?)

9 Have you any advice for the speaker for future talks?

Note: this page can be freely photocopied

FEEDBACK/EVALUATION:

(2) DISCUSSION

1 Was the transition between the presentation and the discussion   SMOOTH/AWKWARD?

2 Generally speaking, was the discussion   LIVELY/RATHER FLAT?   WHY?

3 How many of the group participated in the discussion?   EVERYONE/MOST PEOPLE/ONLY A FEW

4 a) Did the discussion break down at any point, or were there awkward pauses?   YES/NO

   b) If YES, why?

5 How good were the participants at picking up one another's points and taking them forward?   VERY GOOD/GOOD/FAIR/NOT GOOD

6 How was disagreement handled?   WELL/OK/BADLY

   a) Was there a round-up or summary at the end?   YES/NO

   b) If YES, how was it handled?   WELL/OK/BADLY

7 Was there any way in which the discussion could have been improved?

Note: this page can be freely photocopied.

UNIT 6 Managing your studies

This unit aims to help you to:

1. manage your studies more effectively, particularly in relation to your time
2. prepare for exams and other forms of course assessment.

University life

The culture of university is very different from the culture of school, and the culture of a university in one country might be very different from the university culture in another. So whichever of these transitions you make you are probably in for a culture shock!

TASK 1 School to university

Here is a letter written by a student ('Jack') to his friend 'Jim' at the end of his first term at university. What comments have you got on his letter? Have you any advice to give him?

Dear Jim

Well, here I am at the end of my first term. I have to tell you that it's been a bit of an eye-opener for me. The first week was quite good fun – we had "freshers week" where all sorts of fun activities were put on for us. We were also met by other students inviting us to join all kinds of clubs – drama clubs, athletics clubs, political clubs and I don't know what. I didn't know which to join, so in the end I didn't join any. Anyway, I reckoned I was going to be pretty fully occupied with my studies, so I probably wouldn't have time in any case.

The teaching is very different from school. As you know, I'm doing an Arts degree so we only have about 5 lectures a week and two tutorials – only 7 hours work a week. Whoopee! But there's a lot of things I don't like. The lectures are huge – over a hundred students attend each lecture. The lecturers seem to be quite aloof and unfriendly – they don't seem interested in us at all, and give us very little guidance on how we should study, and never seem to check up on how we're doing the way the teachers did at school. I don't know where the first few months of the term went – suddenly the end of term exams seemed to be upon me, and I found myself working through the night to catch up. I've just got some of the results and they are not so good. I don't know whether I'll stick this course. I guess I'll just see how the rest of the year pans out.

Best wishes

Jack

TASK 2 Differences in national university cultures

The article reproduced below, in an edited and shortened form, derives from an interesting (and all-too-rare) attempt to systematically compare the teaching cultures of two highly respected colleges from the students' point of view. The two colleges compared here being the Worcester Polytechnic Institute (WPI), (Massachusetts, USA) and Ingeniørhøjskolen I København (IHK), (Copenhagen, Denmark). The article was written by three WPI Engineering students working with IHK.

1 Read the article then answer these questions:
  a) What do the writers mean by 'traditional' teaching?
  b) In what ways were the teaching cultures of WPI (in USA) and IHK (in Denmark): (i) similar; (ii) different?
  c) Think of an educational institution that you know quite well (either school or university). How similar to/different from the culture of IHK (Denmark) as described here would you say it was?

EDUCATIONAL CULTURES:

A Comparison of WPI [USA] versus IHK [Denmark]

by Erin Gilson, Cara Obadowski, and John Roach

[…]

Before arriving in Denmark, we were under the impression that their classrooms encompassed a very traditional style of teaching, which represents the dutiful listening and note taking of the students while the professor lectures at the front of the class. We have since realized that much of the teaching at WPI is also traditional. […] Furthermore, modern educational innovations usually consist of supplements to the traditional style of teaching. In classrooms at both colleges, the lecture format is generally supplemented with writing on the blackboard, overheads, handouts, and laboratory exercises. Some teachers also use the electronic blackboard to post additional class notes and relevant websites. Essentially, the same percentage of teachers at both institutions utilizes this software. […]

However, while the techniques in conveying the course material within the classroom are very

similar to what we experience at WPI, we did notice some dramatic differences between the educational cultures. For instance, during a meeting with our liaison Knud Holm Hansen, he thought it was humorous that we addressed him as 'Professor Hansen', because a Danish student would most likely use a less formal greeting instead, such as 'Hi Knud.' This represents a variation of cultures, but it illustrates the relaxed environment of the classroom. Claus Petersson, a charismatic professor and helpful contact, enjoys joking with his Math 2 students to keep them involved.

Anders Reichart, a physics professor who was very enthused to assist us in our endeavors, prefers to lead his students through problems solved on the blackboard in colorful chalk and by posing questions to them. This sort of interaction requires the professors to make an effort to know the names of all the students in their course, which is undeniably something that is difficult in many of the larger courses at WPI.

The IHK students have class time as well as conferences for working and solving problems, which is similar to our course structure at WPI. This comparison highlights one of the more prominent differences between the two learning environments. At IHK, a course is divided into two-hour lectures given twice a week and two-hour conference sessions conducted twice a week, for a total of 8 hours in a class. Furthermore, the entire time spent in conference is with the professor who teaches the lectures. During these periods, students work together in groups to solve problems and seek assistance from the professor when they encounter difficulties. When they are not teaching, the professors make themselves easily accessible by remaining in their offices for the students to make further inquiries at their own convenience. On many occasions, we observed that students often visit a professor in his office to simply say 'Hi' and ask how things are going. This presented a refreshing change from the generally constricting office hours of professors at WPI.

These features most likely occur as a result of the relaxed atmosphere of the educational system.

Students attaining a higher education in Denmark receive a free education funded by the country's taxes. In addition, the government provides a monthly stipend of approximately $500 to the students for books, rent, or any other necessity for their education. This setup establishes a less competitive learning environment, because students follow the study programs based on their own initiative.

Overall, we found this atmosphere at IHK intriguing, since we are obligated to pay at least $30,000 a year to 'obtain' a quality education. It is common in America to look for the colleges and the universities that have higher costs, because the level of quality is often equated with the amount spent on one's education.

As our time here in Copenhagen is coming to a close, we reflect on the various differences of the educational cultures. We plan to offer multiple educational innovations to the Export Engineering department at IHK based on our knowledge and analysis of WPI's current programs. However, after extensive interaction with the students and faculty at IHK, we believe that WPI could also benefit from incorporating certain aspects of IHK's atmosphere into their classrooms.

[Source: http://www.wpi.edu/Academics/Depts/IGSD/Perspectives/denmark2.html]

TASK 3 Your teaching culture preferences

1 Below you will find contrasting lists of some ways in which educational cultures can differ. If you are attending or have attended a university in your *home country* put a 'H' above the appropriate part of the line to describe that aspect of its culture. If you are attending a *foreign university* similarly locate it with an 'F'. Put 'ME' underneath the line for *your own personal preference*. So you can use 1, 2 or all 3 symbols, depending on your experience. Taking the first one, for example, let us suppose you have attended a college in your own country where the way to succeed was by memorising lecture notes. You are now in a foreign university where the emphasis is mostly on argument and discussion. You would actually feel more secure if there

was more emphasis on learning some inputs by heart. Then your diagram might look like this:

**Emphasis on
memorisation/rote learning**   **Emphasis on discussion**

H   F

⟵───⟶

ME

Note: This task can be altered to suit your circumstances. For example, if you are currently still at school you can make a contrast between your school culture and what you hope or expect your future college/university culture to be like; if you have moved on from school, you can contrast college/university and school.

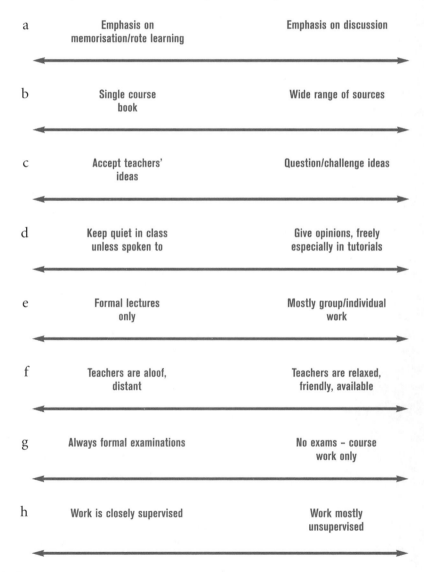

a   **Emphasis on
memorisation/rote learning**   **Emphasis on discussion**

⟵───⟶

b   **Single course
book**   **Wide range of sources**

⟵───⟶

c   **Accept teachers'
ideas**   **Question/challenge ideas**

⟵───⟶

d   **Keep quiet in class
unless spoken to**   **Give opinions, freely
especially in tutorials**

⟵───⟶

e   **Formal lectures
only**   **Mostly group/individual
work**

⟵───⟶

f   **Teachers are aloof,
distant**   **Teachers are relaxed,
friendly, available**

⟵───⟶

g   **Always formal examinations**   **No exams – course
work only**

⟵───⟶

h   **Work is closely supervised**   **Work mostly
unsupervised**

⟵───⟶

i   **Heavy timetable**   **Light timetable**
           Little free time   **A lot of free time**

←———————————————————————————————→

2 *(Group)* If you are working in a group, compare your responses to question 1 with the others' responses. If you have been able to form a view on the college or university you are currently attending, how far do other students' views agree with yours? What about your personal preferences – how far do the other students share your views?

3 *(Individual/Group)* Do you think it is possible for you to change your learning style to suit the culture of the institution you are studying in? How would you go about that? (Remember, every system of teaching and learning has advantages and disadvantages. Try to think of ways in which you can exploit the system in your institution.)

Time management: Study time

You will remember from Task 2 that Jack suddenly realised at the end of the first term that he had very little time to prepare for the end-of-term exams. He didn't know 'where the time went'. This can easily happen if you do not monitor (keep track of) your study time. Look at Study Aid 1, then do Task 4.

Study Aid 1   **Study timetable**

Figure 6.1 is a blank personal timetable, which you have permission to photocopy. You will need to make at least two copies, but probably some spares would be useful. When you start your course, fill in all the times that are 'fixed' such as those for sleeping, travelling, meals and classes. Then fill in the optional activities, for example playing sport, going to the movies, watching favourite TV programmes. Then shade in the time available for private study. How many hours is that in a week? How are you planning to spend that time (for example reading set texts or revising notes)? Fill in the projected use of your study time. Then at the end of the day quickly check on how the day actually went. At the end of the week check over how that week went and, in the light of that experience, make a fresh study-time plan for the next week. If you do that conscientiously, by the end of the term or semester you will (unlike Jack!) at least know where your time has gone.

TASK 4 Time management

- Do you think time management is, or will be, a problem for you?
- Do you think procedures like Study Aid 1 are, or will be, useful in helping you to manage your time?
- Have you any system for prioritising tasks, so that the most urgent and important are done first? (For example some people make lists and cross tasks off as they are done. Others put small re-usable notes [marketed under various trade names like Post-it™ and Sticky Notes™] on a 'To do' board in their study, or on a card which they keep in their diary: these notes can then easily be re-arranged in order of priority and discarded when the task is done.)
- Have you any ideas about how you could save time, so that you will have more time for things that you want or need to do?
- Have you any other ideas about ways in which you could manage your time more efficiently and effectively?

	Monday	Tuesday	Wednesday	Thursday	Friday	Saturday	Sunday	
a.m. 6								6
7								7
8								8
9								9
10								10
11								11
12								12
p.m. 1								1
2								2
3								3
4								4
5								5
6								6
7								7
8								8
9								9
10								10
11								11
12								12

Figure 6.1 Study Aid 1 – Study timetable

Managing assessment

TASK 5 **Some thoughts about assessment**

1 Answer these questions.

   a) In your opinion, is it always the case that students fail exams because they have studied for fewer hours than those who pass?

   b) Apart from the number of hours devoted to study, what are the other factors that decide whether students do well in course assessment tasks?

   c) How important do you think careful planning is in passing a course?

   d) Have you ever done less well than you should in an exam or assessed task because you did not know, or were not sure about, exactly what was required?

   e) If the answer to the previous question was 'Yes', is there anything that occurs to you now that you could have done to get the necessary information?

   f) Is it usually the case, do you think, that all subjects in a course of study are equally important? And within a subject, is it the case that all assessments are equally important?

   g) Is it the case that assessments are evenly spaced throughout the academic year, or do they tend to 'bunch' at particular times of the year? If they tend to bunch, what if anything can a student do about that?

   h) Look at Study Aid 2. Do you think that time spent on this Study Aid would be time well spent? Is there any other information that you think could be added to the Study Aid?

Study Aid 2 **Course assessment outline**

In Figure 6.2 on p. 138, you will find a *course assessment outline* that has been drawn up by a student who is just starting the first year of a degree in Economics. You will see that the student has noted information concerning:

- whether or not a pass in each subject is essential
- the form of the assessment for each subject (e.g. '4 essays, 1 exam')
- the nature of each task (e.g. project, essay)
- in which term or semester the assessment occurs
- the due date of the assessment
- the length of the assessment (e.g. 2,000 words, 2 hr paper)
- the weighting of each assessment (how much it contributes percentage-wise to the final assessment).

You are advised to draw up a similar course assessment outline at the beginning of each academic year. In some courses, such an outline will be provided for you, so all you have to do is study it very carefully.

You are then advised to transfer this information to a work diary (an A5 Academic Desk Diary would be ideal, but any diary will do). In your work diary you should add information as to:

- when assessment tasks are issued
- when you intend to start work on them
- when you intend to finish them. (Note: this may be some time before the task is due, because of the need to avoid *bunching* when several tasks are due about the same time.)

Course assessment outline

1 Statistics   (Must pass)
   weekly class tests
   1 project
   1 exam

Task	Term	Date due	Length	Weighting
weekly class tests	1, 2, 3	(done throughout year)	(not specified)	40%
project	1, 2, 3	21/6	(not specified)	20%
exam	3	26/6	2 x 2 hr papers	
		27/6	(Paper 1 is an open (seen) paper)	40%

2 English language   (Must pass)
   25 weekly exercises, each of equal weight
   No exam

3 Economics   (Must pass)
   4 essays
   1 exam

Task	Term	Date due	Length	Weighting
essay	1	20/11	2,000 words	
essay	2	18/1	2,000 words	
essay	2	20/2	2,000 words	40%
essay	3	20/5	2,000 words	
exam	3	28/6	2 x 3 hr papers	60%

4 Economic history   (Elective subject: pass not essential)
   1 normal essay
   1 essay written under exam conditions

Task	Term	Date due	Length	Weighting
essay	2	22/2	1,500 words	50%
essay/exam	3	20/6	1½ hr paper	50%

Figure 6.2 Study Aid 2 – Sample course assessment outline

Exploiting assessment feedback

Assessing students' work usually takes up a lot of tutors' time, so it is important to take advantage of your tutors' efforts by paying attention to their conclusions.

Most students concentrate on the grade or mark – understandably! But that alone does not always tell you much. Is B a good grade – well, it may depend on how many people got A, C, D ... Is 40% a bad mark? It depends on the class average and on what you need to pass.

TASK 6 Thinking about assessment feedback

1 Answer the following questions.
   a) What kinds of systems of grading or marking have you come across in your studies? Would you say that some are better than others? If so, why?
   b) What are the kinds of things that tutors comment on, in your experience?
   c) Look through Study Aid 3. Are there any ideas there that strike you as being especially useful? Have you any suggestions about other ways of exploiting assessment feedback?

Study Aid 3 Routine for exploiting assessment

- When you get your assignment or test-paper back, note the grade or mark in your work diary.
- Make sure you know what the grade means (in terms of the average achievement of the class, for example).
- Study the tutor's comments carefully.
- What kind of mistakes have you made? Do they relate to the:
  - information (wrong information, not enough, irrelevant)
  - quality of argument (thinking unclear/confused/illogical, lack of evidence, inconclusive, your own position unclear)
  - presentation (untidy, confusingly laid out, references omitted, mistakes in bibliography)
  - style and language (too informal, bad spelling, grammar, punctuation, typos (typing errors))
  - ownership of aspects of the work, that is *plagiarism* (other writers' ideas passed off as your own, sources not properly acknowledged).
- Exploiting the assessment – remedial work can be done in response to mistakes in the:
  - information: check the facts and memorise them
  - argument: make sure you understand exactly where you have gone wrong. Make a checklist for your next assignment
  - presentation: add this item to the checklist
  - style/language: check the facts. If necessary, add it to the checklist
  - ownership of aspects of the work, that is plagiarism: make sure you understand exactly what this term means.

Revision

TASK 7 **The effects of revision**

1 Look at Figure 6.3 and answer the following questions.

a) Which group of children remembered most? Which remembered least? Was the difference between the two groups substantial? How do you account for the differences in achievement?

b) What is the best time for the effort to remember?

c) What do you notice when you compare the rate of forgetting for Group A after the first test (1) with after the second test (2)? What conclusions do you draw from this?

d) Look at Study Aid 4 (Revision routines). How helpful do you think this routine is? Have you any other comments, questions or suggestions about revision?

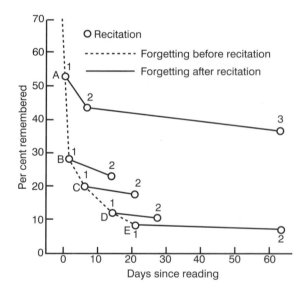

How forgetting is reduced by recitation (i.e. attempting to repeat from memory what one has learned)
Five groups of children (A, B, C, D, E) were given an article to read. Each group was then tested on the content of the article at different intervals. The students were not allowed to revise the article and were not given the correct results of the tests. The curve therefore shows the effects of simply *trying to remember.* (Diagram adapted from Deese 1964, after Spitzer, 1939

Figure 6.3. References:
Deese, James (1964) *Principles of Psychology* (Boston: Allyn & Bacon)
Spitzer, H.F. (1939) 'Studies in retention'. *Journal of Educational Psychology,* 30: 641–56.

Study Aid 4 Revision routines

- There is evidence that about 80 per cent of what is learned may well be forgotten unless revision/recitation takes place. Even if you don't have time to sit down and revise, the simple act of *trying to remember* ('recitation') will substantially help remembering.
- Most forgetting takes place within 24 hours. So try to revise new material on the same day – the sooner, the better!
- The more frequently revision/recitation is done, the more slowly forgetting takes place. Revise frequently.
- Don't leave revision to just before the exams. By that time you will actually have to relearn much of the material, which will take much more of your time than if you had revised it promptly.

Remembering

TASK 8 Techniques for memorising

We have seen in this book that there are many aspects to successful study – being able to read efficiently, to do basic research, and so on. The ability to memorise is obviously very useful too, especially where exams are concerned. Also, some subjects (such as Medicine) seem to require more use of memorisation than others.

1 a) Read over the sequence of numbers below. Starting at the beginning of the top line, try to remember the numbers by reading them slowly in groups of three. You have one minute to do this. Then close the book and see how many of the numbers you can write down.

      2 9 3 3 3 6 4 0 4 3 4 7
      5 8 1 2 1 5 1 9 2 2 2 6

  b) Now do the same task again – but this time look for some system in the numbers. Here is a clue: start on the *bottom* line.

  c) What have you learned from doing these tasks?

2 Look at Figure 6.4, which is a one-page diagram summary of the text *Malaria – a new threat* (for the original text, see Unit 1, Task 5). Some students think it is helpful to make diagrammatic summaries like this when they want to remember information. Can you think of any reasons why making one-page diagrammatic summaries like this might help memorisation?

3 Look at Study Aid 5, and then answer these questions.

  a) Are there any memorisation techniques here that you already use, or that you think you might want to use?

  b) Are there any memorisation techniques *not* mentioned here that you have found useful?

c) Look at the section on Mnemonics later in this unit. Three exceptions to the spelling rule are listed. Can you think of a mnemonic to remember them?

d) Have you read/visited any useful books or web sites on improving your memory? (If you would like some suggestions on useful books/web sites, see the Appendix.)

Study Aid 5 Memorisation routines

- Whenever possible, after a lecture, tutorial, lab session, reading of a text for example, try to quickly go over in your mind what the main points were – use recitation frequently.

- Set aside a period every working day (at least 20 minutes) when you will quickly revise the notes and reading you have done during the day.

- You are unlikely to remember what you don't understand. Before you attempt to memorise something, first make sure that you understand it.

- Reduce the amount you have to learn by concentrating on main ideas and essential facts.

- Organise your material in a concise way, by using one-page diagrammatic summaries for example.

- Relate the things you want to learn to one another, and as far as possible also to your own life and thoughts.

- If there are lists of things that you have to learn off by heart, or two names/technical terms that you keep confusing, try to associate them in some meaningful way such as by using a mnemonic. (See below.)

Mnemonics

Mnemonics are techniques for remembering specific pieces of information.

The first thing to remember is that the letter m in mnemonic is silent! The word is pronounced /ni'monik/.

Here are some of the many different ways of using mnemonics.

By making up a rhyme

(The example below is used in English, to remember the spelling of words like brief, *believe, deceit* and *receive* which are spelled using the letters *ie* or *ei* with the pronunciation /i:/)

> *i* before *e*
> except after *c*

(Some common exceptions to this rule are: *weird, seize, counterfeit.*)

By using the number of letters in a word to represent an actual number
(The example below is used in Mathematics, to remember $\sqrt{2} = 1.414$. The first line gives the answer to the second. This mnemonic also uses rhyme.)

> I wish I knew
> The root of two

By using the initial letters of the words to be memorised
(The example below is used in Biology, to remember the parts of an insect's leg, namely the coxa, trochanter, femur, tibia, tarsus and claw.)

> *C*ockroaches *t*ravel *f*ast *t*owards *t*heir *c*hildren.

(This is probably the most popular kind of mnemonic, because it is usually easy to make up. This example is especially good because the meaning of the sentence closely relates to the meaning of what is being memorised.)

(*For discussion.* Can you think of any other ways of memorising facts/details? Do you have a favourite method?)

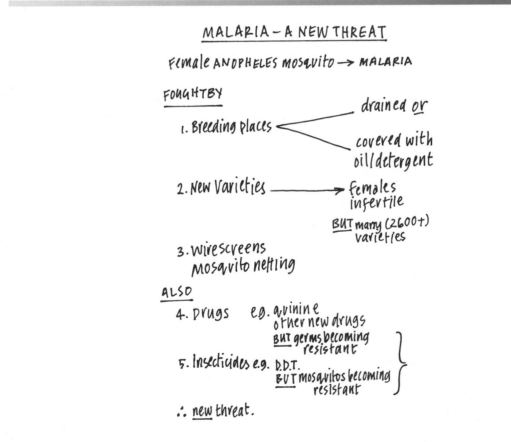

Figure 6.4 Study Aid 5 – Diagrammatic summary

Preparing for examinations

Most courses of study, especially at undergraduate level, involve sitting examinations. (Not all courses, though – if you are one of the lucky ones who does not have to sit an exam, then you can skip this final section!)

TASK 9 **Thinking about exam preparation routines**

1 a) How do you feel about formal examinations? Do you think they are a good way of assessing students' achievement?

   b) Look through Study Aid 6 (Preparing for examinations). It summarises advice that is usually given to students on this topic. How useful and practical do you think the advice is that is given there? Is there any advice there that you will probably not follow? Why?

   c) Have you any suggestions of your own about preparing for exams?

   d) Now look at Study Aid 7 (Day of the examination routine). How useful/practical do you think this advice is? Is there any advice given here that you would probably ignore?

   e) What about your own routine for examination day? Are there procedures that you find especially helpful?

Study Aid 6 **Preparing for examinations**

- Find out the details of the time, date and place of the examinations. Make a careful note of them in your work diary and highlight them.
- Nearer the time of the examinations, double-check the details.
- For each examination, find out:
  - the length of the examination
  - how the paper is organised
  - the number of questions on the paper
  - how many questions you have to do
  - the nature of the questions (e.g. essay or multiple choice).
- Decide on how long you are going to allow yourself for each question.
- Make a list of the questions you think you might be asked.
- Prepare a one-page diagrammatic summary for each question you might be asked.
- Prepare an exam revision timetable, especially noting study hours per day.
- If possible, make sure all major revision is completed two days before the exam. Keep the last day for a quick overall revision.
- Try to get a reasonable amount of rest on the night before the examination.

Study Aid 7 **Day of the examination routine**

- Get up in plenty of time.
- Make sure that any equipment you need (pens, calculators, etc.) is
  - in working order
  - located where you cannot possibly leave it behind in a last-minute rush.
- There should be no last-minute rush! You will be at a great psychological disadvantage if you arrive late, or even just in time.
- When you are allowed to look at the exam paper, check through the rubric (instructions) carefully. There may have been changes since the last examination.
- Be sure about the number of questions you have to do, and check whether any questions are compulsory.
- Tick the questions you intend to do. Decide when you ought to have ended each question. Note the time down beside the question.
- Allocate some time at the end (up to five minutes) for checking over the paper.
- Start with the easiest question. If it is an essay-type question jot down ideas in any order that they occur to you. You may find it useful to use branching notes at this stage. Organise your notes. You can spend between 10 and 15 per cent of your time on this planning stage.
- Do each of the questions in turn, ending with the one you feel least confident about.
- Watch your time, and make sure you write something on each question.
- If you have run out of time, it may be useful to write your answer, or part of it, in note form.
- Quickly check through the paper. If any words seem difficult to read, write them out again more clearly.

Appendix: Some useful study resources

Checklist:

Human resources
- Teaching staff
- Librarians
- Study advisers
- Fellow students
- Study groups
- Student organisations
- E-mail contact

Library resources
- Catalogues
- Databases (BIDS, Index to Theses, etc.)
- Journals (to find relevant/useful references)

Web-based resources
- Search engines
- Subject guides
- Multiple database subject guides ('Virtual libraries')

Internet research guides

Style manuals
- Your college/university style guide
- MLA Handbook
- APA Publication Manual
- and more

How-to-study books

Reference management software

Human resources

Don't forget that, above all else, colleges and universities are (or should be) 'people places': sometimes your most valuable learning resource will prove to be those working and studying with you.

- *Teaching staff.* An obvious source of help and advice. Teaching staff are after all the people who will assess you, so no one else is better placed to give you good advice and point you in the right direction.
- *Librarians.* Another obvious resource. If they can't give you the information you need, they should have ideas on where to find it.
- *Study advisers.* Most universities have advisory services which are intended to help students with all aspects of university life, including their studies.
- *Fellow students.* Perhaps we normally think of our fellow students as a distraction from study rather than an aid to it! But students can help one another in many ways, for example by forming informal study groups, by sharing ideas or sources, by proofreading one another's essays just before submission, and so on. One danger to avoid, of course, is excessive collaboration that may be seen by tutors as a form of cheating.

- *Student organisations.* As well as being a source of recreation and relaxation (an important aspect of any university life), student clubs and societies may be a valuable source of intellectual stimulus, for example by inviting guest speakers to speak on relevant topics.
- *E-mail contact.* This is an alternative way of making contact with tutors, other students and even relevant people outside the university. Of course, if you are communicating with someone you do not know, particularly from outside the university, e-mail has to be used with care, tact and discretion. Any responses you get may be reliable or they may not, depending on who sent them. You will find more detailed information on the use of mailing lists and so forth in Internet research handbooks (see, for example, N. O'Dochartaigh (2002: Chapter 4). Full reference below under *Internet Research Guides.*)

Library resources

Your first port of call when you are researching an assignment will probably be the library of your college or university. Most libraries are very good at introducing students to the range of their facilities, and most will have helpful computer-based search facilities to help you find your way through the college/university catalogue. University computerised catalogues will usually also give you access to databases of sources that may or may not be in the university library, but which can usually be obtained through it, for example by using inter-library loan.

Examples of databases include:
- BIDS (Bath Information and Data Services) (http://www.bids.ac.uk) BIDS provides access to a range of databases. It is freely available to UK university users, but some of its databases are accessible outside the UK too.
- ISI's Web of Science (http://www.isinet.com) This database concentrates on articles that are cited or quoted in other articles. In this way important articles in various disciplines are highlighted. (Also available for registered users through http://wok.mimas.ac.uk)
- The UK Joint Information Services Committee (http//www.jisc.ac.uk) provides a useful series of 'Resource Guides' in the areas of: Arts and Humanities/Engineering, Mathematics and

Computing/Geography and the Environment/Health and Life Sciences/Hospitality, Leisure, Sport and Tourism/Physical Sciences/Social Sciences.

- There are dozens more databases – your university or college catalogue or subject guides should lead you to the ones that are relevant and accessible to you.
- It is sometimes helpful to check whether there are any articles relating to your research topic in recent issues of journals held in the library. The articles themselves should be helpful, of course, but the bibliography or list of references at the end of an article may be of even more use to you.

Web-based resources

There is a vast variety of web-based resources available through the Internet, but be careful – you can get lost out there! You can also waste a lot of time wandering round looking at material that can be fascinating but that is using up your limited study time to no immediate benefit.

It is usual to make a distinction between two kinds of resources:

- search engines
- subject guides.

(However, in practice, as we shall see, these two kinds of resources overlap in various ways.)

Search engines

In some ways search engines are very easy to use – almost too easy. You simply type in the topic you are interested in and see what comes up. (Usually too much …) We have already looked at one of the best-known search engines, Google (http://www.google.com), in some detail in Unit 3. As we saw in Unit 3, one of the big problems with search engines is handling and focusing the amount of information that is thrown up.

If you don't get what you want in the first few pages of your search results, it might be an idea to have a quick look at another search engine and try it. There are many possibilities. Here are a few:

- Altavista (http:altavista.com)
- Hotbot (http://www.hotbot.com)
- Ask Jeeves (http://www.askjeeves.com) This site operates by answering 'plain language' questions like 'What is the capital of France?'.

There are also so-called 'meta-search' engines which search through several search engines at the same time. However, at the time of writing these are considered to be rather blunt instruments, not recommended for the beginning researcher.

Subject guides/subject indexes

A subject guide or subject index may focus in on a particular subject or it may attempt to cover all the major fields of knowledge (universal subject guides). Library classification systems like the Dewey Decimal System or the Library of Congress system are basically universal subject guides, as they try to include all actual and possible areas of human knowledge.

There are many commercial universal subject guides available such as Yahoo! (http://www.yahoo.com/). Sometimes, however, you will find that these can contain advertising material that is quite intrusive.

Let us take as an example a non-commercial universal subject guide which is maintained by volunteer editors: the dmoz Open Directory Project (http://www.dmoz.org). Let us say that you are a biology student who is researching an essay on plants that can grow in desert areas. The Open Directory is divided into broad areas of human knowledge/interest such as Arts, Business, and Science. Clicking on Science will bring up further sub-divisions (Biology, Psychology, Physics). Biology will lead you to Ecology, then to Ecosystems, then to Deserts, then to Desert Plants.

Alternatively, if you do not want to browse through the categories, you can simply use the guide like a search engine by typing in the specific topic in which you are interested.

Multiple database subject guides ('Virtual libraries')

There are also several subject guides which can access multiple databases. One of the best of these at the time of writing is the Internet Public Library [IPL] (http://www.ipl.org) run by the University of Michigan School of Information. This is an excellent facility for all students, which is extremely 'user-friendly'. It is what it claims to be – a virtual public library. Like all good public libraries, it has special sections for children and teenagers, a comprehensive reference section, a reading room with books, magazines and newspapers, and subject collections. These subject collections also provide access to substantial databases. To give only one example, through the 'Regional and Country Information' collection, those interested in Asian Studies can access the very comprehensive 'Asian Studies WWW Virtual Library' organised by The Australian National

University. In its 'TeenSpace' section, the IPL also has helpful features for young and beginning researchers on basic research techniques together with a list of 'Searching tools', guides to library classification systems and so on.

Internet research guides

Where can you get useful information on using the Internet for your research? First of all, remember that the best place to start from is always your own college or university. It may be that there are published or on-line guides available from your own local sources, so, if they are available, check out those first.

As you would expect, some of the most helpful guides to doing research on the Internet are available on the Internet itself. As we have noted above, web sites like the Internet Public Library can lead you to useful sources and even online tutorials. There are many other sources you can find through search engines like Google. Useful examples are:

- http://www.useekufind.com ('You seek, you find')
- http://www.sofweb.vic.edu.au (site run by the State of Victoria Department of Education and Training, Australia)
- http://library.albany.edu/internet (site run by the library of the University at Albany, USA)
- http://www.vts.rdn.ac.uk (site run by the Resource Discovery Network, funded by the UK Joint Information Services Committee. Highly recommended: this is a very user-friendly site, and even provides separate tuition for several different subject areas).

There are also many book guides. One example:

- Niall O' Dochartaigh (2002) *The Internet Research Handbook: A practical guide for students and researchers in the social sciences* (London: Thousand Oaks/New Delhi: Sage Publications). As the sub-title indicates, this is primarily aimed at students in the social sciences, but that should not put students in other disciplines off. The topic is explored more comprehensively than in most books of its kind. It is also very clearly written.

There are many other guides, some directed at first-year students, but they tend to have, quite naturally, a local bias or are sometimes concerned with a specific subject area. The best idea would be visit your local university bookshop or check out a bookseller web site like http://www.Amazon.com using key words like *Internet* and *student* or *Internet* and *research*.

Style manuals

You may want more detailed information on the presentation of papers and assignments than can be provided in an introductory text like this one.

- As usual, the best place to start is with any guidelines provided by your own tutors. Your college or university may also provide a guide on what writing and presentation conventions are acceptable.

- There are also published style guides, often related to specific subject areas. Examples are the *MLA Handbook for Writers of Research Papers* (New York: The Modern Language Association of America) and the *Publication Manual of the American Psychological Association* (Washington, DC: American Psychological Association). No publication date has been given for these as, like many such manuals, they are regularly updated. You will want to use the most recent one, if it is available, as it is more likely to have up-to-date information on references to electronic sources and so forth. The American Psychological Association provides regular updates on changes made for the most recent edition at its web site (http://www.apastyle.org), which also gives style tips, answers queries and provides the latest information on using electronic references within the APA guidelines. If you are using the Modern Language Association (MLA) system you will find a very helpful and regularly updated guide prepared by Capital Community College (Hartford, Connecticut, USA) at http://webster.commnet.edu/mal/index.shtml.

How-to-study books

There are literally hundreds of books on how to study, some of them specialising in particular areas of study, particular areas of academic work, or particular levels of study (undergraduate/postgraduate). Here are a few good examples:

BELL, Judith (1999). *Doing Your Research Project: A guide for first-time researchers in education and social science* (3rd edn). Buckingham/Philadelphia: Open University Press.

COLLINS, Sylvie C. and Pauline E. KNEALE (2001). *Study Skills for Psychology Students: A practical guide.* (London: Arnold/New York: Oxford University Press)

COTTRELL, Stella (1999). *The Study Skills Handbook.* (Basingstoke/New York: Palgrave)

NORTHEDGE, Andrew, Jeff THOMAS, Andrew LANE and Alice PEASGOOD (1997). *The Sciences Good Study Guide.* (Milton Keynes: The Open University)

All the above books are basically concerned with relaying good advice in an accessible and motivating way. If you prefer the more 'task-based' approach used in the present book, then you should find the following companion titles to the present one of use (all are published by Cambridge University Press):

GLENDINNING, Eric H. and Beverley HOLMSTRÖM(2004) *Study Reading: A course in reading skills for academic purposes.*

HAMP-LYONS, Liz and Ben HEASLEY (2004) *Study Writing: A course in writing skills for academic purposes.*

ANDERSON, Kenneth, MACLEAN, Joan and LYNCH, Tony (2004) *Study Speaking: A course in spoken English for academic purposes.*

LYNCH, Tony (2004) *Study Listening: A course in listening to lectures and note-taking.*

Reference management software

If you are fortunate enough to have access to and use of what is sometimes called 'reference management software', then it may be worth your while devoting some of your precious study time to learning how to use it. By using this software, you can download references from bibliographies and Internet sources, have them arranged and printed in whatever way is required by the style guide you are using, insert references into your document and search for the references using pre-selected keywords. Some reference management systems available at the time of writing are: *Biblioscape, Citation 7, Endnote, GetARef, Idealist, Procite, Reference Manager.* Most comprehensive reference management systems are expensive and are usually accessed through institutions. However, it may be worth noting that at the time of writing there is a freeware version of Biblioscape which can be run from a floppy disk. It is called BiblioExpress. (Please note that *Biblioscape* systems do not run on Macs.)

Information about any of these systems can be found through Google: simply type in the name of the system you are interested in, followed by the keywords *reference management system.*

UNIT 1 Key

TASK 1

1 Examples of possible answers: there are dozens of possible reasons for reading! It could be because:
   a) you want to pass the time
   b) you usually enjoy books in that genre (e.g. detective novels, science fiction, biography)
   c) the book is on your course booklist
   d) it was recommended by your tutor
   e) it should give a general idea about a new subject, a kind of introduction to the subject
   f) you can use it to find out some information that might help you with an essay that you are writing
   g) there is a particular section or article in it that might be useful
   h) you've read other books by the same author and found them very interesting
   i) because you've read a review of the book in a magazine/journal that highly recommended it
   j) because you came across it in the library when looking for another book and thought it might be useful/relevant.

2 Academic reasons: c), d), e), f) and g), possibly also b), h), i) and j).

3 Purpose for reading and the way a book is read: There should be a connection! For example, if you are reading for a specific piece of information, you will want to find the relevant part of the book as quickly as possible. If you want to get a general idea of what a book is all about, this will involve a very different approach. How you change your way of reading to suit your purpose in reading is one of the key topics of this Unit.

TASK 2 **Global warming and extreme weather: a cautionary note**

Examples of possible questions:
- Is the world actually getting warmer?
- Will this cause the weather to be more extreme?

Summary

Many people believe that the world is getting warmer, and that this will result in more extreme weather conditions. However, there is no clear statistical support for this. Also we suffer from a lack of data. Outside the US and some countries in Western Europe, extreme weather conditions have been recorded only for about the last 20 years or so. Even where climate change has been monitored for long periods, no consistent trend in weather variability that can be related to global warming has been found.

Six billion and counting: trends and prospects for global population at the beginning of the twenty-first century

Examples of possible questions:

- Is the world population still growing at the same rate as it did in the past?
- Will this process continue into the future?

Summary

The world's population has doubled in the last sixty years. In the last twelve years alone world population has increased by a billion. On the other hand, annual population growth rates have been slowing, from over 3.0 per cent in 1960 to 1.4 per cent currently. The increase in population is caused by an unprecedented decline in mortality levels owing to: improvements in sanitation and hygiene, improved health care, higher living standards and improved disease patterns. Factors in the decline in fertility include: access to and use of contraceptives, the education of children and mothers, and also decreased child mortality. Parents tend to have fewer children when they are confident their young ones will survive. So although world population will continue to grow, it should do so more slowly than in the recent past.

Unconstrained growth: the development of a Spanish tourist resort

Examples of possible questions:

- What happens when the growth of tourist resorts are not constrained or regulated in any way?
- How should tourist resorts be developed?

Summary

Like many other Spanish tourist resorts, Torremolinos experienced explosive development and growth in the period 1950–1990. Much of the tourist provision during this period (high-rise hotels etc.) was done in an uncontrolled way to maximise income from the boom in tourists. This frequently resulted in an ugly environment, which made the resort potentially unattractive to the more discriminating tourists of the 1990s. Improvement of the town's environment is therefore now a top priority and steps have already been taken to achieve this.

Age concern? The geography of a greying Europe

Examples of possible questions:

- Is the population of Europe getting older, and if so, by how much?
- If the population is getting older, is that a problem? In what way?

Summary

The population of Europe is getting older. It is estimated that by 2025, nearly 30 per cent of the population of the European Union will be aged 60 years or over. The increase in the number of elderly people poses problems for governments in terms of increased social security budgets and increased need for health and social care. The objective for the future has to be to enable older people to enjoy an active and independent life for as long as possible, and to maximise support for those who need it in the final stages of their lives.

Changing responses to water resource problems in England and Wales

Examples of possible questions:

- How serious are the water resource problems in England and Wales?
- What can be done to solve these problems?

Summary

The water industry in England and Wales is now in private ownership. It is faced with a forecast shortage in its basic resource in some places because of population increase, increased demand for water, and possible climatic change. It also may be approaching the limits of its resource in certain areas, so that any extra water will have to come from outside. Various solutions have been considered, e.g. the control of waste caused by leakage, but no single solution will be enough. Overall, a balanced approach is required between the control of demand and the increase of supply.

TASK 3

1 *Author's academic position.* Michael Argyle is Emeritus Reader in Social Psychology at Oxford University, a Fellow of Wolfson College, and Emeritus Professor of Psychology at Oxford Brookes University. [*Emeritus* is an honorific title given to distinguished academics that allows them to keep their academic titles (e.g. *Professor*) even after they have retired.] He is obviously very well qualified to write with authority on Psychology.

2 *Date of publication/updating.* The book was first published in 1987, but this is the second edition, published in 2001. In the preface, the author tells us that, since the first edition, 'I have been carrying out research and writing on some of the central topics of the present book, and this has helped me rewrite some chapters.' We are also told in the publisher's blurb that: 'Major research developments have occurred since the publication of the first edition in 1987 – here they are brought together for the first time, often with surprising conclusions.' The blurb also informs us that: 'New to this edition is additional material on national differences, the role of humour, money, and the effect of religion.'

3 *Audience/needs of target audience.* The blurb tells us that the book will be 'compulsive reading for students, researchers and the interested general reader'. Given the author's academic background, he should be experienced in knowing the needs of students and researchers.

a) *Suitability for beginning students of Psychology.* According to the blurb, the book is comprehensive and up-to-date, and this view is echoed in the reviews quoted from Professors Robinson and Furnham. Professor Diener says that the book gives a 'broad overview', it is 'interesting' and 'exciting' but 'not a difficult read.' He also says that Argyle does an outstanding job of introducing readers to the field. All this makes it sound suitable even for beginners.

b) *General reader: happiness.* You would probably want to read Chapter 13 ('Happiness enhancement').

c) *Economics student.* Probably Chapter 7 ('Work and employment') and Chapter 9 ('Money, class and education').

TASK 4   **Note:** subheadings are indicated by the + sign.

1 [health and happiness]
- **Main references: health**, 43f, 219f; + behaviour, 81; + relationships, 87f; **mental health**, 15, 220f; + and relationships, 86f; **neuroticism**, 15, 152f, 180f, 187, 193
- **Also:** dopamine [chemical released by brain], 35; drugs, 38f, 212f; endorphins [chemicals released by brain], 35; General Health Questionnaire (GHQ), 16; heart attacks, 80, 110f, 116; immune system, 87; neurotransmitters, 35f; Prozac [a drug], 36, 202, 213; religion + effect on physical health, 169, + effect on mental health, 171; religious beliefs + healing, 170; serotonin [chemical released by brain], 35

   (You might also have found other references relevant, depending on how widely you interpret the term 'health'.)

2 [economics]
- **Main references: income**, 132; + comparisons with, 140f; + dispersion, 186; **job satisfaction**, 87f, 96f; + measurement of, 89; + new technology, effects of, 93; **money**, 43, 131f, 222; + interest in, 184; + symbolic value of, 143; **pay**, 91f, 105, 108; + rises, 138; **work**, 89; + and unemployment, 44, 89f, 224; + health, 101f; + performance, 217; + social aspects of, 93; + stress, 101
- **Also:** class differences, 205; employment, 44; job control, 92f, + nature of, 92f; unemployment, 103f

   (As before, you might also have found other references relevant, depending on how wide your interests are.)

3 [earnings] there is an entry under **income**

4 [sunny] there is a reference under **weather** to page 33, where a source is quoted as saying (surprise!) 'people are in a better mood when the sun is shining…'

5 [countries]
- **Main references: national differences**, 178f, 226; + income, 137, 183; + measurement problem, 180f; + economic changes, 138f; **happiness**, + national differences in, 4, 17f
- **Also:** Britain, 195, 197f; Jewish humour, 67; USA, 189, 195f

TASK 5   1 (various answers)

2 You should have been able to see that, according to the writer, dangerous new developments are taking place involving increasing resistance to modern drugs and to insecticides.

3 a) Two ways: marshes pools, etc. were drained; areas of still water were covered with oil or detergent.

   b) A different variety of mosquito is introduced. When the two varieties mate, the females are infertile.

c) Three methods: use of wire screens/netting/protective cream or spray; taking of protective drugs like quinine etc.; use of insecticides.

d) Two methods: malaria germs are becoming more resistant to modern drugs; mosquitoes are developing a resistance to DDT.

TASK 6

1 Various answers are possible, but 'language' and 'the Internet' would seem to be safe bets! Also 'linguistic revolution' seems to be implying some kind of important or drastic change in language, perhaps caused by the invention of the Internet?

2 Main points
- the Internet is a linguistic revolution
- misspellings etc. not revolutionary
- revolutionary aspects of Internet are:
  – framing
  – web pages are a new medium of communication that is like writing but not permanent
  – chatrooms allow one to 'listen' and 'speak' to dozens of people at the same time
  – what started as an English-only medium has become truly multilingual.

3 **Summary**

The Internet is a linguistic revolution. It consists of several domains, including e-mails, the World Wide Web, chatrooms (both virtual and real), and fantasy games. With e-mails, the fact that they are often written in an inaccurate and idiosyncratic way is not truly revolutionary. What is revolutionary is the possibility of framing, which allows Internet users to split up messages they receive which can then be sent on to other people and further split up and so on. With regard to Web pages, the revolutionary thing is a kind of writing which is not permanent. Web pages can change in front of your very eyes. Chatrooms offer the possibility of 'listening' and speaking' to dozens of people at the same time in a way that has never been possible before. Lastly, another revolution in the Internet is the way it has changed from an English-only medium to a truly multilingual medium. [151 words]

TASK 7

1 [acupuncture]
a) endorphins are morphine-like substances contained within the brain tissues. (They therefore can give feelings of peace and tranquillity and freedom from pain.)
b) Acupuncture originated in China. It has been used there for over 3,000 years.

2 [Canary Islands]
a) The Canary Islands are 100 kilometres (60 miles) off the North-west coast of Africa.
b) False. According to the Roman writer Pliny the Elder, the islands got their name from the many dogs found on them (the Latin word for dog is *canis*).

3 [family]
  a) The nuclear family consists of husband, wife and children living together ('co-resident'). The extended family consists of grandparents, uncles, aunts, cousins, etc., who do not necessarily live in the same house ('non-resident').
  b) In England and the USA most of the population no longer live in nuclear families: only about 20% of the population now live in nuclear families.

TASK 8

1 [Outline notes]
Topic: <u>Language and the Internet</u>.

1 Internet is a <u>linguistic revolution</u>

2 There are several <u>domains</u>:
  – e-mails
  – World Wide Web
  – chatrooms
  – fantasy games
  a E-mails
  – way written (bad grammar etc.) NOT revolutionary
  – FRAMING (splitting up messages) IS revolutionary
  b Web pages
  – can change in front of your eyes
  c Chatrooms
  – can 'speak' and 'listen' to dozens of people at same time.

3 Change from English-only medium to <u>multilingual medium</u>

2 [Diagram notes]

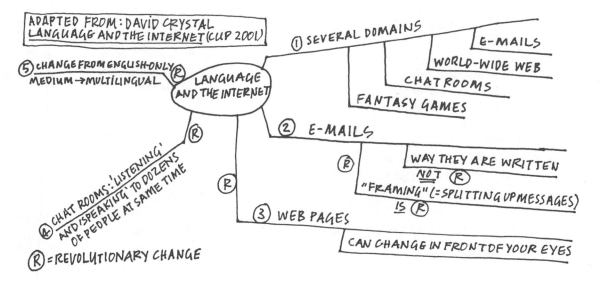

TASK 9   1 *Prediction*: Various answers, but clearly it will be something to do with the ways in which men and women experience pain. It also seems to be saying that the ways in which the two sexes experience pain are very different.

2 *Skimming*: main topics. Topics include: painkillers affect men and women differently; why these differences have not been spotted earlier; biological reasons for different pain thresholds between men and women; implications of different pain thresholds.

3 *Searching*

a) John Levine made the surprising discovery that certain strong painkillers (kappa opioids) were very effective with women, but did not work for men at all.

b) *Reasons why different reactions to drugs by men and women have eluded scientists for so long*: (any three of the following) (i) there are many different aspect to pain (it is 'multidimensional'); (ii) pain is a highly subjective phenomenon; (iii) pain varies with different factors (e.g. time of day, age of sufferer); (iv) until recently, drugs were tested only on men; (v) even now test-results for drugs are not differentiated according to sex.

c) *Possible biological explanations for different reactions of men and women to pain*: (i) men and women tend to suffer from different disorders because of their different physical make-up; (ii) even when the source is the same, men's and women's brains may handle the pain differently; (iii) men tend to be more stoical about their pain (at least in public) – they seem to have a higher pain threshold.

4 a) Check your reading speed using the Reading speed chart.

b) *Summary*

Possible answers:

1 painkillers shown to affect men and women (m+f) differently
   e.g.   KAPPA OPIOIDS (only helped f.)
          IBUPROFEN (only helped m.)

2 Why not discovered <u>before</u>?
   – pain is <u>multidimensional</u>
   – pain is highly <u>subjective</u>
   – pain <u>varies</u> according to age/diet etc.
   – drugs used to be tested only on m
   – results don't separate m and f

3 Why does pain affect m + f differently?
   – m + f suffer from <u>different disorders</u>
   – m + f biochemistry, nerve connections, brains <u>handle pain differently</u>
   – men more stoical, have <u>higher pain threshold</u>

4 Women may <u>live longer</u> because they react to pain <u>more quickly</u> and <u>seek help sooner</u>

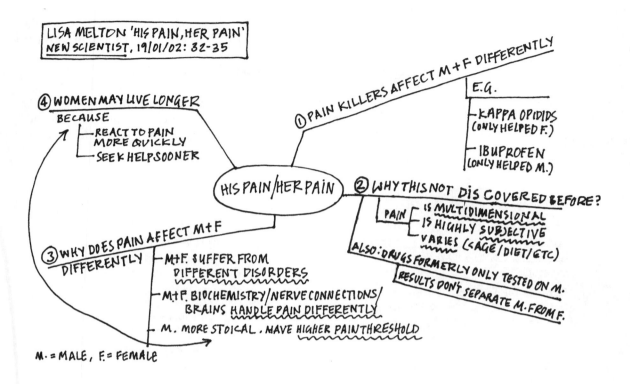

LISA MELTON 'HIS PAIN, HER PAIN'
NEW SCIENTIST, 19/01/02: 32-35

④ WOMEN MAY LIVE LONGER
BECAUSE
┌─ REACT TO PAIN MORE QUICKLY
└─ SEEK HELP SOONER

① PAIN KILLERS AFFECT M+F DIFFERENTLY
E.G.
┌─ KAPPA OPIOIDS (ONLY HELPED F.)
└─ IBUPROFEN (ONLY HELPED M.)

HIS PAIN/HER PAIN

② WHY THIS NOT DISCOVERED BEFORE?
PAIN ┌─ IS MULTIDIMENSIONAL
     ├─ IS HIGHLY SUBJECTIVE
     └─ VARIES (<AGE/DIET/ETC)
ALSO: DRUGS FORMERLY ONLY TESTED ON M.
RESULTS DON'T SEPARATE M. FROM F.

③ WHY DOES PAIN AFFECT M+F DIFFERENTLY
┌─ M+F. SUFFER FROM DIFFERENT DISORDERS
├─ M+F. BIOCHEMISTRY/NERVE CONNECTIONS/ BRAINS HANDLE PAIN DIFFERENTLY
└─ M. MORE STOICAL. HAVE HIGHER PAIN THRESHOLD

M. = MALE, F. = FEMALE

TASK 10 [Prediction: Study the title]
1 a) Among other things, economists are concerned with how material wealth is produced, maintained and distributed.
  b) Among other things, environmental scientists are concerned with how our external surroundings affect our lives, and how those surroundings can be maintained or improved.
  c) Ecologists believe that the most important thing is maintaining and improving the environment, whereas economists have to be concerned with how much those activities will cost and whether we can afford them.
2 [Establishing your own position]
[various answers]
3 [Skimming: Answer to the title question]
According to the writer, economists argue that everything must have a value 'in dollars and cents', but environmentalists deny that the environment can always be reduced to a cash value.
4 [Scanning: Philip Graves' paper]
According to Graves, people might be willing to work harder to pay for environmentally-friendly goods, and therefore pay more for them than economists at present calculate on the basis of what people are earning just now.

5 [Careful reading]
    a) [Structure of text] (i) *Problem.* Environmentalists cannot agree with economists that all environmental issues can be reduced to a cash value. (ii) *Proposed solution* (Graves). Increase the cash value of environmental issues by about 10%. (iii) *Evaluation of the solution.* It does not resolve the conflict because environmentalists will never agree to any upper limit to what must be spent on saving the environment. Also, while people in rich areas may be willing to find the extra 10% cash to protect the environment, those in less well-off areas may not.
    b) Summary

[*The Economist,* 02/02/02, p 82]

<u>Never the twain shall meet: Why do economists and environmental scientists [= e.s.] have such a hard time communicating?</u>

Reasons for conflict:

1 ECONOMISTS say everything (including environment) can be valued in cash terms
E.S. say envt cannot and shd not be reduced to cash value
(BUT writer says choices will always have to be made)

2 ECONOMISTS say <u>values</u> must dictate <u>policy</u>
E.S. say <u>policy</u> must come first

How do we establish VALUE?

– SAMUELSON: value = what people are willing to spend (BUT how do you discover this?)
– GRAVES: people might be willing to work harder to pay for envt: perhaps as much as 10% more (BUT less well-off may not be willing to pay so much more for envt)

Writer's conclusion: Graves' solution will not resolve conflict, because e.s. will never agree to put an upper limit on value of envt.

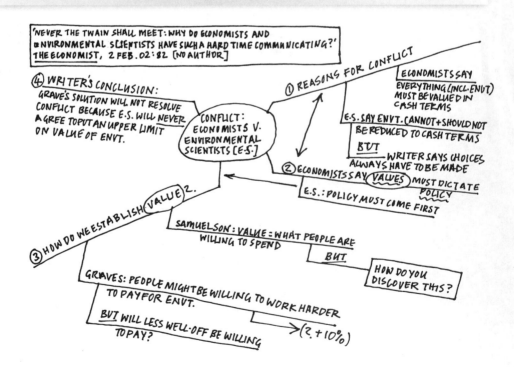

TASK 11

1 [Prediction: title]
The title seems to indicate that it is possible to protect the planet and by doing so generate wealth.

2 [Establishing your own position]
(Various answers)

3 [Scanning: Costa Rica]
Costa Rica plans to shift entirely to renewable energy by 2025.

4 [Searching: name three countries that have done something to bring about a sustainable environment]
- 31 countries in Europe + Japan: stabilised population
- China moving towards population stability
- Denmark: stabilised population/banned construction of coal-fired power plants/banned use of non-refillable beverage containers/15% of energy from wind/restructured transport network/32% of all trips in Copenhagen by bicycle
- South Korea: reforestation programme
- Costa Rica: will shift entirely to renewable energy by 2025
- Iceland: plans to be world's first hydrogen-powered economy.

5 [Careful reading]

a) (i) *the problem*: At present, the global economy is being shaped by market forces, not by the principles of ecology. This is creating an economy that is destroying its own natural support systems.

(ii) *proposed solution*: convert the present economy into an 'eco-economy', i.e. one shaped by the principles of ecology.

(iii) *The three main areas of the economy that will be affected by an 'eco-economic' approach are*: energy supply; use of (raw) materials; and food production management.

b Summary

'Save the planet (and prosper)' [Lester Brown, The Ecologist, 31/10 Dec 01/Jan 02: 26–31]

1 Global economy at present shaped by market forces NOT by principles of ecology. This has created an economy that is destroying its own natural support systems.

2 Converting present economy into an 'eco-economy' will be a monumental task.

3 Nevertheless already some progress being made esp. in stabilised populations (31 countries in Europe, plus Japan, and China getting there). Best example is Denmark (stable population, renewable energy, recycling, use of bicycles), also South Korea (reforestation), Costa Rica (renewable energy by 2025), Iceland (plans world's 1st hydrogen-powered economy).

4 Restructuring the economy:
a) ENERGY: from oil/coal/natural gas to wind/solar cells/geothermal energy
b) MATERIALS: from linear model (mine/forest to landfill) to reuse/recycle model
c) FOOD: better management of 'natural capital' (stabilise aquifers/conserve topsoil/increase land productivity/conserve forests).

5 Results: Companies that plan for the new eco-economy will prosper, those that don't, may not.

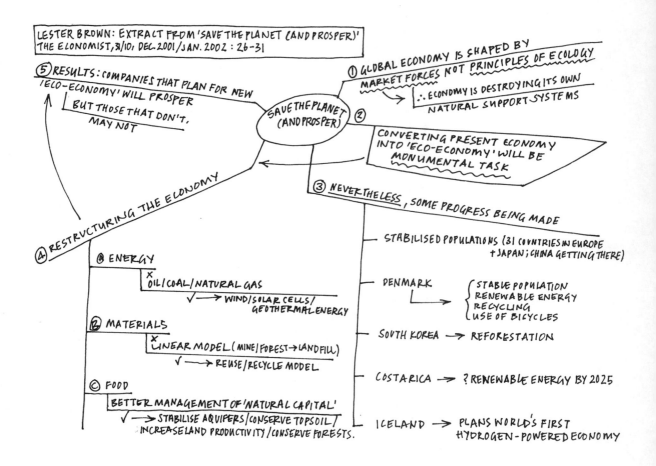

LESTER BROWN: EXTRACT FROM 'SAVE THE PLANET (AND PROSPER)'
THE ECONOMIST, 3/10, DEC. 2001/JAN. 2002: 26-31

⑤ RESULTS: COMPANIES THAT PLAN FOR NEW
'ECO-ECONOMY' WILL PROSPER
BUT THOSE THAT DON'T,
MAY NOT

SAVE THE PLANET
(AND PROSPER)

① GLOBAL ECONOMY IS SHAPED BY
MARKET FORCES NOT PRINCIPLES OF ECOLOGY
→ ∴ ECONOMY IS DESTROYING ITS OWN
NATURAL SUPPORT-SYSTEMS

② CONVERTING PRESENT ECONOMY
INTO 'ECO-ECONOMY' WILL BE
MONUMENTAL TASK

③ NEVERTHELESS, SOME PROGRESS BEING MADE

④ RESTRUCTURING THE ECONOMY

ⓐ ENERGY
✗
OIL/COAL/NATURAL GAS
✓ → WIND/SOLAR CELLS/
GEOTHERMAL ENERGY

ⓑ MATERIALS
✗
LINEAR MODEL (MINE/FOREST → LANDFILL)
✓ → REUSE/RECYCLE MODEL

ⓒ FOOD
BETTER MANAGEMENT OF 'NATURAL CAPITAL'
✓ → STABILISE AQUIFERS/CONSERVE TOPSOIL/
INCREASE LAND PRODUCTIVITY/CONSERVE FORESTS.

— STABILISED POPULATIONS (31 COUNTRIES IN EUROPE
+ JAPAN; CHINA GETTING THERE)

— DENMARK ⎰ STABLE POPULATION
⎱ RENEWABLE ENERGY
RECYCLING
USE OF BICYCLES

— SOUTH KOREA → REFORESTATION

— COSTA RICA → ? RENEWABLE ENERGY BY 2025

— ICELAND → PLANS WORLD'S FIRST
HYDROGEN-POWERED ECONOMY

UNIT 2 Key

TASK 1 **Discussion**

Many people would immediately think of a learning resource which is featured in this Unit – namely, lectures. But there are some courses in which lectures do not play a prominent part. In some courses, seminars and tutorials are equally important. In others, for example science courses, performing or observing experiments or practical tasks is also very important. In distance learning or 'open university'-type courses, inputs through the media (such as television, radio and the Internet) form an essential part of the study process. It is also important not to overlook more informal and less programmed ways of learning: student study groups, discussing ideas or problems with fellow students, questions put to tutors, comparing notes with fellow students after a lecture, and so on. How important these are to you will depend, among other things, on the way your course is organised, on the kind of person you are and the way you prefer to study, and on your relationships with your fellow students. However, whatever conclusions you have come up with now for Task 1, it is important not to get into a rut and, as your studies progress, always to be on the look-out for ways in which you can learn more efficiently and perhaps more enjoyably.

TASK 2 **Discussion**

The point was made earlier that one reason for taking notes is to help our memory. Sometimes it is very important to *remember something exactly*, so we note it down. Examples of things that we want to remember exactly are people's telephone numbers, e-mail addresses, postal addresses and so on – so these things are usually noted down carefully. Thinking of academic studies, if we see something in a book or article that we think we might want to quote, then we have to be careful to note it down accurately. We would similarly want to take careful note of the source details, for example getting the author's name exactly right, and also details of the book or journal.

But it is not always possible or even desirable to note down everything exactly. If you are listening to a lecture, unless you are skilled at shorthand, it is not possible to record the speaker's every word – and even if you could, you might not want to. You will probably be more interested in the main points or the general drift of the lecture. Or there may be one part of the lecture that you feel is more relevant to you than others. In these cases you have to be more selective. Such note-taking may actually be a way of interacting with the input: trying to make sense of it, trying to record its relevance to you. This kind of interaction with the input makes it more likely that you will be able to remember it, and to use it to good effect.

TASK 3 (Possible answers)

1 **Writing down every word from source**
Advantages: No information lost – complete record.
Disadvantages: Time-consuming. You may not have time to think about what the speaker is saying and interact with it. May be frustrating unless you use some form of shorthand. Probably unnecessary – usually it is the speaker's main ideas you are interested in, not the actual words used.

2 **Using outline (linear) notes**
Advantages: Very straightforward method. Concentrates on the main ideas. Allows you to interact with the speaker's message (you have to think about the message before you can choose what you think is worth noting).
Disadvantages: Some detail may be lost.

3 **Using diagrams/branching notes**
Advantages: Concentrates on the main ideas. Allows you to interact with the speaker's message. Display may help you to make sense of the speaker's message, and also remember it more easily.
Disadvantages: Some detail may be lost. Technique may not always be convenient to use. Technique does not appeal to everyone.

4 **(Text) Underlining/highlighting in colour**
Advantages: Easy and quick to use.
Disadvantages: Cannot be used on library books/journals.

5 **(Text) Computer scanning**
Advantages: Easy and quick to use. Text can be saved and edited.
Disadvantages: Requires specialised equipment (computer, scanner, printer). Also requires some computer expertise.

6 **(Text) Photocopying**
Advantages: Easy and quick to use. Text can be filed for future reference and highlighted etc.
Disadvantages: Can be expensive if used extensively. Does not require interaction with the text: photocopying a text is not the same as studying it!

7 **(Text) Making notes in margins**
Advantages: Easy and quick to use. Encourages interaction with the text.
Disadvantages: Cannot be used on library books/journals. Comments may be disorganised, not easily accessible.

8 **(Spoken input) Audiorecording**
Advantages: No information lost – complete record. Can be supplemented with notes taken from the input.
Disadvantages: Speaker's permission may have to be sought. Time-consuming – not as easy to scan as written notes.

1

Abbreviation	Meaning
e.g.	for example
etc.	and so on
cf.	compare
et al.	and others (often used to mean other authors)
ibid.	in the same place (in a book or article)
N.B. *or* n.b.	note well (something important)
viz.	namely, that is to say

2

Meaning	Symbol
is equal to, the same as	=
is not equal to, not the same as	≠
therefore, thus, so	∴
because	∵
plus, and, more	+
minus, less, except	−
greater than	>
less than	<
much greater than	≫
much less than	≪
at least equal to or greater than	≥
per cent	%
divide, divided by	÷
multiply, multiplied by	×
insert (something that has been omitted)	⋏
from…to, leads to, results in	⇒

Pyramids

Pyramid = grave of an Egyptian king, Old + Middle Kingdoms (2680 - 1567 BC)

Earliest P. built for K. ZOSER (= 'step P.' (because) sides go up in large steps; 197 ft (60m) high

Largest P. is one of a gp of 3 built at GIZA, s.th of CAIRO. by Kings of the 4th dynasty (2680 - 2525 BC). Called the 'Great P.' built by K. KHUFU (GR = CHEOPS). Outside of P. = 2m. + blocks of stone. Av. weight of each block = 2·5 tons (2,540 kilos)

2 [Malta]

Malta

Malta = 3 islands (MALTA, GOZO, COMINO)
M. island = 95 sq miles (246 sq. km.)
GOZO = 26 sq miles (67 ")
COMINO = 1 sq mile (2·7 ")
Est. pop of M. = 363,000 (as at 2000)
Capital = VALETTA : magnificent harbour
Maltese lang. mainly ← Arabic + many Sicilian wds
Major industries = tourism, ship repair
M. is v. imp. shipping centre for Mediterranean

TASK 6
1 *The End of Age.* Something to do with old age coming to an end. Perhaps the idea that people will live forever?
2 *Brave old world: 'We are programmed for survival'.* Seems to suggest that nature has designed people to live (for ever?) rather than dying at a particular maximum age.
3 *Making choices: 'Choices matter to older people'.* Perhaps the speaker will suggest that old people should be able to make choices, to have control over their lives. Perhaps also that governments, or younger people, can make choices which will impact on older people, for good or ill.
4 *New Directions.* Future developments of some kind. Perhaps ways of getting old people to extend their life span, or to improve their quality of life?

TASK 7

Discourse marker	Function
From the time of	TIME
Not only...but also	ADDITION
Since	CAUSE & EFFECT
Yet	CONTRAST
because	CAUSE & EFFECT
For instance	EXAMPLE
Then, too	ADDITION
If	CONDITION
Thus	CAUSE & EFFECT
Eventually	TIME
Finally	LISTING
even though	CONTRAST

TASK 8
1 a) Any one of these discourse markers for LISTING:
   firstly   secondly   lastly.
   b) Any six discourse markers for CAUSE AND EFFECT:
   this means that   it will be obvious that
   clearly   obviously
   so   hence
   it follows that   therefore
   as one might expect   thus
   because.
   c) Any two discourse markers for EXAMPLE:
   let us take the case of   let's say
   examples   to take one good example.
   d) One discourse marker for CONTRAST:
   nevertheless.
   e) One discourse marker for DEFINITION:
   in other words.

f) Two discourse markers for CONDITION:
unless   provided that.

g) One discourse marker for SUMMARY
(what I've been saying) amounts to this.

9.1   **Listing** (discourse markers are shown in **bold**, the function of each
is given after both passages)
Topic area: Management studies
Title: Role stress in organisations
One of the complaints most frequently heard among workers these
days has to do with being stressed, and I would like to deal with
some aspects of this topic today. There are many possible causes of
stress in the workplace. One of these has been identified by the
management expert Charles Handy as ROLE STRESS.

What do mean when we speak of a person's role? In this context,
a person's role is the part played by him or her in an organisation as
manager, secretary, salesman or whatever. Sometimes, stress is
caused by what Handy calls ROLE AMBIGUITY – that is,
uncertainty in the minds of the people working in the organisation
as to the precise nature of their role in that organisation.

According to Handy, the four most frequently cited instances of
role ambiguity in a work situation are:

Firstly, uncertainty about *how one's work is to be evaluated* (that is,
judged or assessed). What are the methods or procedures that are
being used to assess my worth to the organisation?

Secondly, uncertainty about *scope for advancement*. Is promotion
possible? If so, what does one have to do in order to be promoted?

The third thing is uncertainty about *scope for responsibility*. What
things am I responsible for, and what things are part of someone
else's responsibility?

And **the last thing** is uncertainty about other people's *expectations
of one's own performance*. What is it that my colleagues and my
superiors expect of me?

I think you can see how uncertainty about these issues could easily
cause stress and anxiety.

(Based on material to be found in Charles B Handy (1981) *Understanding
Organisations* 2nd Edn (Harmondsworth: Penguin Books))

9.2   **Contrast** (discourse markers are shown in **bold**, answers given after
this passage)
Topic area: Language studies
Title: Speech and writing
The two main means of language communication are, of course,
speech and writing. For many people, writing is simply speech in

another medium. **However, although** these two important language media share many common characteristics, **they also differ** in many significant ways.

Of course, it is true that [write-] writing ultimately derives from speech, and in that sense speech has a primary place. **But** writing is more than speech in another form. It has its own unique characteristics.

One of the most important differences between speech and writing is that speech is much more time-bound. By that I mean that most spoken interaction takes place when the speaker and the listener are in communication at the same time. (**The main exception** to this occurs with recorded messages.)

With the written word, **on the other hand**, there is almost always a gap in time between the writer writing the message and the reader receiving it. This means that the writer has much more control over the form of the message than is usual in speech. Greater care can be taken, and the message may even go through several drafts. This can have important implications for the nature and the range of the vocabulary and grammatical features used.

Another important difference related to time is that usually speech has to be processed during the time that the message is being spoken. For example, a student listening to a lecture usually has no control over the lecturer's speed of utterance. With a written text, **the opposite is the case**. The reader can read the text at his or her own pace, either quickly or slowly. Also, it is an easy matter to read again parts of the text, or indeed all of it, if necessary several times. So we see that the language skills necessary for listening to a spoken input can be **very different from** those required for reading a written text.

Discourse function and discourse markers used

- LISTING   Firstly; secondly; the third thing; the last thing
- CONTRAST However; although; they also differ; But; one of the most important differences; the main exception; on the other hand; another important difference; the opposite is the case; very different from…

9.3

Discourse function	Possible note-taking strategy
LISTING	use numbers (1,2,3…); take new line for each item in list
CAUSE AND EFFECT	use 'therefore' sign (∴); use 'because' sign (∵); use arrow sign (⇒) to mean 'causes'
EXAMPLE	e.g.; ex.; exx. ('examples')
CONTRAST	use BUT; list contrasting items in two columns; use tick (✓) for 'the same as' and cross (✗) for 'is different from'; v. (= versus, 'against')
TIME RELATIONSHIP	use arrow(s) to denote 'was followed by'

9.4 a) LISTING input
[Role stress in
organisation]

<u>Role stress</u>

Role = part played in organisation
— ROLE AMBIGUITY
① uncertainty about <u>how one is</u>
<u>evaluated</u>
② — <u>about advancement</u>
③ — <u>responsibilities</u>
④ — <u>others' expectations</u>

b) CONTRAST
input [Speech
and writing]

<u>SPEECH and WRITING</u>

S. and W. differ — W. is not just S. in another
form
① S. is time bound
W. — writer has more control
② S. has to be processed while it is being
spoken
W. — reader can take time/read again

TASK 10   *[Audio inputs]

10.1   **Emphasis** (discourse markers are shown in **bold**, the function of
each is given after the two passages)
Topic area: Study skills
Title: Learning and remembering
Wouldn't it be wonderful for us as students if we could remember
everything?
    Actually – no!
    It would be a disaster. We would be drowned in information and
be unable to function. So, in preventing us from having total recall,
nature is actually doing us a favour. In everyday life we filter out
most of the experience data available to us and we select what is
important to us.
    But how can I make sure that I will remember the things I need
to remember? Let's start with a very obvious point, which is paying
attention. Unless we are aware of something and *paying attention* to
it, there is no way that we will remember it. **This is an important**

point, but often easier to acknowledge than to put into practice. A common example is when we are introduced to people for the first time. We know we should remember the names of people we meet but our attention is deflected perhaps by observing our new acquaintance or thinking of something to say, and so we don't properly register their name. Some experts recommend therefore that we repeat the person's name ('Hi, Jim, nice to meet you!'), or even make some kind of mental image linking the person's name to his or her appearance. These are basically just ways of paying attention.

During an extended input like a lecture or a seminar it is sometimes very difficult to keep up our level of attention. So it is **extremely useful to** interact with the input in some way. We can do this, for example, by making notes, writing down questions we'd like to ask, noting where we disagree with or we are not sure of what the speaker is saying and so forth.

Another factor in memory of course, is revision. **The key point here is** that the sooner the revision is done the better. Research seems to indicate that most forgetting takes place very soon after the input has taken place.

Thirdly, **and this I would say is a crucial issue** for most study purposes – is that what we are trying to remember *must be meaningful to us*. It must make sense to us, and if possible we must be involved with it in some way. The rote learning of lots of isolated facts is not usually a very efficient method of learning. If the meaningfulness is not easily found in the material to be learned then somehow or other we have to impose meaning on it. We have to think about it until we have discovered some meaningful shape or pattern to it.

10.2 **Summary** (discourse markers are shown in **bold**, the function of each is given after this passage)

Topic area: Psychology

Title: Emotional Intelligence

In a University environment like this, I guess that few personal attributes are more highly valued than intelligence. After all, it's a person's intelligence, powers of reasoning, cleverness – call it what you will – that opens the door to academic advancement. In this talk, however, I'm going to discuss the view that perhaps the concept of intelligence that most people carry around in their minds is too rigid and narrow. Perhaps there are actually different kinds of 'intelligence'. In particular, I would like to focus on one kind of intelligence which falls outside the widely accepted definition of what it means to be intelligent. This is the quality which the writer David Goleman has popularised as 'emotional intelligence'.

Goleman argues that in the past there has been a tendency to value pure reasoning above other aspects of human character as the key to success. It's almost as if the ideal model of the human mind was some kind of superfast computer. However, this model downplays the fact that our emotional development is of crucial importance to healthy living and even to success in our careers. Goleman gives many examples of people who are very intelligent intellectually but whose success in life has been fatally undermined by a kind of emotional inadequacy.

What is emotional intelligence, then? One researcher, Peter Salovey, suggests that emotional intelligence denotes abilities in five domains:

Firstly, *knowing about our own emotions*, that is self-awareness about our feelings. If we are not aware of the role of feelings in our lives, then we are at the mercy of those feelings.

Secondly, *the ability to manage our emotions*. This means that we have developed strategies for consciously changing our moods, or at least lessening the negative effects of moods that are harmful to ourselves or those that we relate to.

Thirdly, *being able to motivate ourselves to control our [emo-] emotions*. We may do this, for example, by delaying gratification, that is by putting off something we want to have or to do, because we have a long-term aim that requires this kind of self-discipline.

Fourthly, *the ability to recognise emotions in others*. This is sometimes called *empathy*, and simply means being sensitive to other people, to their reactions in social situations and to their feelings.

Finally, *the ability to handle relationships*. If we are in charge of our own emotions and sensitive to the feelings of others, then we can motivate other people to work with us and we relate well to them. The ability to handle human relationships is a key element for success in many areas of life.

It is Goleman's belief that our emotional character is not just a 'given', that is something unchangeable that we have to live with. He believes that, just as academic development is trained and developed at school and higher education, so too emotional development can be similarly trained and developed from an early age – what he calls 'schooling the emotions'.

To sum up, the view that has been discussed here today is that emotional intelligence is just as important for success in life as the reasoning kind of intelligence that can be measured by IQ tests and so forth. Further, we have noted the argument that an individual's emotional intelligence is not a 'given', something static and unchanging, but on the contrary something that can be improved, trained and developed.

Reference: Daniel Goleman (1996) *Emotional Intelligence: Why it can matter more than IQ* (London: Bloomsbury)
Peter Salovey's definition of emotional intelligence is described in Goleman, pp. 43–44.

Discourse function and discourse markers used

- EMPHASIS This is an important point; it is extremely useful to…; The key point here is; (and this I would say) is a crucial issue
- SUMMARY To sum up

10.3

Discourse function	Possible note-taking strategy
6 EMPHASIS	use block capitals underline draw box around point
7 REPHRASE/DEFINITION	use 'equals' sign (=) i.e.
8 ADDITION	use 'plus' sign (+) use numbers
9 CONDITION	if…then…
10 SUMMARY	use box to contain summary

10.4 a) EMPHASIS
input
[Learning and
remembering]

Learning and Remembering
(NOT a good idea to be able to remember everything!)
① Pay attention (eg. names - repeat name/mental
    image)
    - interact with input
      (eg. notes/questions)
② Revision
    - sooner the better
*③ Must be meaningful, we shd. be involved

b) SUMMARY
input
[Emotional
intelligence]

EMOTIONAL INTELLIGENCE
    - Different kinds of intelligence
      → Emotional intelligence
        [best human mind = computer?
        NO - v. intelligent people
          intellectually can fail
          in life]
↳ ① self-awareness
  ② Manage one's emotions/moods
  ③ Motivate ourselves to control emotions/moods
  ④ Recognise emotions in others (empathy)
  ⑤ Handle relationships
* GOLEMAN believes E.I. can be developed/trained

TASK 11 *[Audio inputs]

Note: discourse markers are shown in **bold**, the function of each is given at the end of the input. A tabulated answer to Task 11 is also provided at the end of this section.

Extract 1   Subject area: Politics

When a party is elected to Parliament in Britain it cannot stay in power for more than five years without calling an election. But – and **now this is the important point** – the Prime Minister may 'go to the country', that's to say, call an election at *any time* before the five years are up. This is important because it gives the Prime Minister in Britain a lot of power – he or she can choose the best time to have an election for their own party. In many other countries, the timing of an election is fixed – it must take place on a certain date every four years, or whatever. This means that in these countries the President or Prime Minister can't choose the most convenient time for him or herself the way a British Prime Minister can.

Function: Main point

Extract 2   Subject area: History of Medicine

One of the most dramatic examples of the effect of advances in medical knowledge is the building of the Panama Canal. In 1881, work was started on building this canal under the supervision of Ferdinand de Lesseps, the Frenchman who built the Suez Canal. The project had to be abandoned after the mosquito-borne diseases of yellow fever and malaria had claimed 16,000 victims among the workers. Some twenty years later, the area was made healthy by spraying the breeding waters of the mosquitoes with petroleum. Work was able to be started again in 1904 and the canal was finished in 1914.

Function: Example

Extract 3   Subject area: Sport

By the way, since we have mentioned the Olympic games, you may be interested to know the following curious fact about the ancient Olympic Games as compared to the Modern Olympics. The ancient games were held every four years without interruption for over a thousand years. The modern games have already been cancelled three times (in 1916, 1940 and 1944) because of world wars.

Function: Digression

Extract 4   Subject area: Zoology

Although it is not strictly speaking relevant to our topic, perhaps I might say something about sharks since they are in the news quite a lot these days. Sharks have got a very bad reputation and probably most people think that all sharks are killers. This is not the case. In fact the largest sharks of all (I mean the Whale Shark and the Basking Shark) are usually harmless to man.

Function: Digression

Extract 5   Subject area: Research methods.

In this talk on the survey method of research, I am going to deal with the topic under four main headings.

Firstly, I'll deal with some preliminary considerations, namely: the purpose of the enquiry, the population to be investigated, and the resources available to carry out the research.

Then, I'll go on to discuss some issues related to sampling. such as sample size, sampling error and so on.

The third topic will be the design and management of questionnaires.

And finally, I will deal with the processing of survey data.

Function: Overview

Extract 6   Subject area: History of Science

A good illustration of how scientific discoveries can be made accidentally is the discovery of penicillin. Alexander Fleming was a bacteriologist who for fifteen years had tried to solve the problem of how to get rid of the disease-carrying germs or microbes in the human body without causing any dangerous side effects. Fleming was an untidy worker and often had innumerable small dishes containing microbes all around his laboratory. One day, one of the dishes was contaminated with a mould, due to the window having been left open. Fleming noticed that the mould had killed off the microbes, and it was from similar moulds that the miracle drug penicillin was developed. Of course, only a brilliant scientist like Fleming would have been able to take advantage of this stroke of luck, but the fact remains that the solution to his problem was given to him, literally, on a plate.

Function: Example

Extract 7   Subject area: Language study

So, in this talk I've tried to make clear the differences that some linguists have drawn between an accent and a dialect. An accent is usually held to be a feature of how the language sounds mainly in terms of pronunciation, how sounds are pronounced. A dialect is basically determined by the vocabulary and grammatical expressions used. **I've also pointed out that** a dialect, particularly a standard dialect, can be spoken with a variety of accents, but it is also often the case that a particular regional dialect of a language will be spoken with a characteristic accent.

Function: Review

Extract 8   Subject area: Psychology

What I want to emphasise to you is this: that people remember things that make sense to them or which they can connect with something they already know. Students who try to memorise what they cannot understand are almost certainly wasting their time.

Function: Main point

No.	Function	Discourse marker	Worth noting?*
1	Main point	Now this is the important point	1
2	Example	One of the most dramatic examples	3
3	Digression	By the way	4
4	Digression	Although it is not strictly speaking relevant to our topic	4
5	Overview	In this talk on the survey method of research, I am going to deal with the topic under four main headings	1
6	Example	A good illustration	3
7	Review	So, in this talk I've tried to make it clear I've also pointed out that	1
8	Main point	What I want to emphasise to you is this	1

*Worth noting? – suggestions only.

TASK 12 (Linear notes for 'The rise and fall of DDT')

Rise and Fall of DDT (source: Isaac Asimov: 20th Century Discovery)

① Since WW2 (39-45), DDT used in large amounts
— crops saved
— insect-spread diseases almost wiped out

② BUT
— upset balance of nature
— some insects were naturally resistant to DDT
— eventually almost EVERY species of insect developed resistance
— DDT could also poison birds/fish

ORIGIN AND FUNCTION OF MONEY
- Different people produce different things eg. farmer/carpenter

- Simplest means of exchange is BARTER
  └ BUT only works in very simple societies

- Anything can act as money if everyone agrees on its value

- Money should have certain qualities
  - convenient
  - durable
  - rare

BUT some exceptions have been recorded

2 Branching notes for 'The origin and function of money'

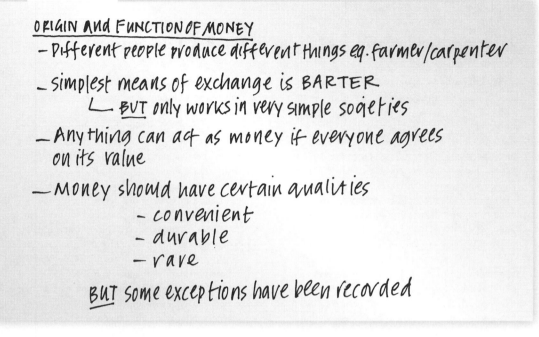

Note: for the mini-lectures, suggested answers are given only for Task 14 question 2 and Task 15 question 2 (note-taking tasks) since the other tasks require individual answers.

Learning styles and strategies in Higher Education

Today I'm going to talk about learning styles and strategies with particular reference to people like you who are studying or about to study at university. This may not be something you've thought about consciously but you probably have specific things you do when you're studying which you feel help you to learn. There has been a large amount of detailed research into the methods people use to learn effectively and I want to try and make sense of some of it for you today.

First I'll look at some of the theories that psychologists have put forward about the way people learn. I'm not going to go into great detail because I've given you some references that you can follow up after the lecture so I'll just outline some of the different theories that psychologists have proposed.

Now, these theories fall into two broad categories: one looks at study behaviour and analyses what successful and less successful students do. The other looks at different personality types and the kinds of teaching required for them to learn effectively. The assumptions [lying -] underlying much of this research are that if students are made aware of their study behaviour then it should be possible for them to change to more effective ways of studying. And similarly if teachers are made aware of students' learning styles they can adapt their teaching methods to suit.

So the implication underlying the research is that people are not prisoners of one particular learning behaviour or style. In fact you probably already use different styles in different learning situations without being aware that you do this. The research suggests that people tend to have a preference for one style over another but as they move through their university career that can change. For this reason it is probably better to think in terms of learning strategies which people can choose for different kinds of learning

tasks rather than learning styles. It is important not to pigeonhole people by suggesting they only have one learning style.

So I hope that by the end of this lecture I will have raised your awareness of different learning styles and strategies which might help you make more effective use of your study time.

So, what do we mean by *learning styles?*

Well, they've been defined as simply the different ways in which people prefer to learn. Researchers have observed different learning behaviours and they have also designed sets of questions to try to identify different personality types and their approaches to learning.

One distinction that researchers have drawn is between syllabus-bound and syllabus-free learners. Now what does this mean? The syllabus, of course, is the list of items that will be taught in a course so a syllabus-bound learner is probably a person who likes to know exactly what is in the course and what they are required to do. They are probably not likely to read widely outside the set course books and they need exams in order to study. They expect a lot of guidance. Their attitude is 'Tell me what to do and I'll do it'.

Syllabus-free learners, on the other hand, don't like too much structure to the course. They prefer being able to choose what they want to study and they work better when they can follow their own interests.

Another kind of distinction considers how active students are in seeking information about their [stu-] studies. Researchers have classified students as being cue-seekers or cue-conscious or cue-deaf. Now the term *cue* might be unfamiliar to you. It usually means the words which signal that it is someone's turn to talk, especially in the theatre. The way it is used in this study is a little bit different from that. Lecturers often give cues about their courses, or in other words, they give important information about timetables and examinations that will help the students with the different stages of the course.

Cue-seekers then seek out or look for these cues. They are very active in trying to find out what is expected of them on the course. They will ask very specific questions about how they can get good marks in essays and examinations, for example. Cue-conscious learners are not as pro-active as cue seekers. They will notice if the tutor gives tips about the exam but they don't try to ask specific questions to get this information. Cue-deaf learners are not sensitive to this kind of information from the tutor at all and because they are not consciously aware of what the course requires they may not do as well as they should.

So this three-way distinction is really about how sensitive people are to the requirements of their course.

Another distinction is between serialists and holists. Serialists like to do one thing at a time. They work from the bottom up by learning individual bits of information and then putting the whole thing together to try to make sense of their studies. Holists work in the other direction. They prefer to have an overview of a subject, for example, so they can understand the Big Picture, and then they can gradually fill in the things they don't know. So, in reading, for example, serialists and holists would have quite different strategies for understanding the text. Serialists might need to read slowly and understand all the words before they could understand the meaning, while holists would skim over the text quickly to get the Big Picture and ignore anything they didn't quite understand to begin with.

The final example of a learning style which I want to talk about today under the category of study behaviour is the distinction between deep and surface approaches to learning. Researchers have defined deep processors as people who engage actively and critically with a text or a lecture. These people ask questions such as 'Do I agree with this?' and 'Does this fit in with what other lecturers have said about this subject?' They have the confidence to relate what they are reading to their own personal experience and to question whether an author's conclusions are justified by the evidence presented.

In contrast, surface processors tend to memorise the facts in a text so they can produce them in an exam. They are often unable to remember afterwards what the text was really about.

So just to sum up this part of my talk, I've been giving you examples of study behaviours and you can perhaps already see that in each of the two- or three-way distinctions I've mentioned there is one behaviour that probably leads to more successful learning than the others. The most successful learners tend to be those who are active in their learning. They are interested in what they are learning and are prepared to go beyond the syllabus. They actively question, both their lecturers and their course materials, and they look for the Big Picture to get an overview of how the whole course fits together.

In the next part of the talk I want to look briefly at learning styles in terms of personality types. Now, it's important to say here that we are not saying that one personality type is better than others for effective learning. Rather we are recognising that because people have different personality types they will have different learning styles. Lecturers and tutors who are aware of these differences use a range of different teaching strategies for different types of learner. However, learners can experiment with different styles to find those that are most useful for different tasks.

One very popular distinction in learning styles is between visual learners, auditory learners and kinaesthetic learners. These relate to the three main ways that we receive information: through sight or hearing or movement. (So *kinaesthetic* is the movement one.) This kind of learning style is forced on us to some extent by traditional schooling. In our early years new information is usually given to us through movement. Later, the main way we receive information is visually and it's only at college and university and then in our working lives that this changes to auditory input through lectures, for example.

Now, a more sophisticated theory is Kolb's *Learning Style Inventory* which recognises that learning needs to be active and based on experience. This inventory uses a model with two dimensions which you can see in the diagram. The first dimension runs horizontally and is based on the task. So, the left-hand side is for doing the task (or performing) while the right-hand side is watching somebody else do the task (observing). The second dimension runs vertically across the first and is based on thought and emotion. So, the top of the dimension is feeling while the bottom is thinking.

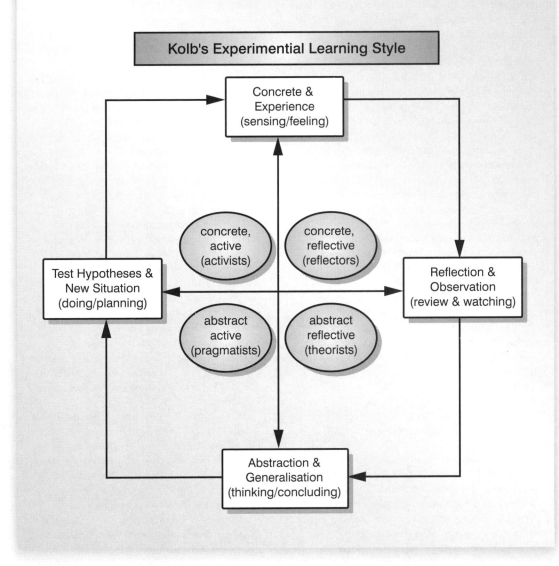

Kolb's Experimental Learning Style

Concrete & Experience (sensing/feeling)

concrete, active (activists)

concrete, reflective (reflectors)

Test Hypotheses & New Situation (doing/planning)

Reflection & Observation (review & watching)

abstract active (pragmatists)

abstract reflective (theorists)

Abstraction & Generalisation (thinking/concluding)

Now you can see that these lines intersect each other and form four quadrants which give us four personal learning styles.

Theorists in the bottom right-hand corner like to learn by thinking and watching. **Pragmatists** like to learn through practical application of ideas. **Activists** in the top left-hand corner like to involve themselves immediately in new experiences, while **Reflectors** like time to think about the subject.

So if we consider how each of these learners might approach learning to ride a bicycle we might find that Reflectors would think about riding and watch someone else ride a bike; Theorists would want to have a clear understanding of the biking concept; Pragmatists would want some tips and techniques from a biking expert and Activists would just jump onto the bike and have a go.

Kolb's Inventory is actually two models in one, a four-step learning process – watching, thinking, feeling and doing – which is then used to describe four learning styles: Reflectors, Theorists, Pragmatists and Activists. These are not discrete categories because learners might find themselves at different places along the task line or the thinking/feeling line so their personal learning style might be a mixture of styles. They might also choose a different learning style for different tasks.

To sum up then, I've talked today about different styles of learning. In the first part of my talk I focused on research which looked at effective study behaviour; and in the second part I looked at research which classifies learners' personality types.

Learning is a very complex process and none of these theories and models can really describe it completely because each one has to simplify the process in a different way in order to begin to understand it. Of course it is interesting to analyse our learning styles but as I mentioned earlier it is important to remember that no one is a prisoner of their learning style and people can and do change the way they learn.

The consensus from all these studies is that the most effective learners are active learners. If you are excited by what you are learning; if you are prepared to go beyond the designated syllabus to follow your own lines of research; if you go beneath the surface to question what you are learning and why, then it is likely that you have a successful learning style.

[Mini-lecture – Outline notes]

Linear notes

LEARNING STYLES AND LEARNING STRATEGIES

Theories of learning
- ① Study behaviour
- ② Different personality types

NB People are not "prisoners" of their learning styles
better to think of strategies

Learning styles

most successful students are ACTIVE + go for the BIG PICTURE

(1) syllabus-bound (need guidance)
syllabus-free (prefer freedom to choose)
(2) cue-seekers – actively seek out info. about course
cue-conscious – are aware of info.
cue-deaf – don't notice
(3) Serialists (bottom-up readers)
holists (go for the big picture)
(4) deep (active/critical)
surface (memorise text)

Personality types
(1) visual (sight)
auditory (sound)
kinaesthetic (movement)
(2) KOLB'S Inventory (see diagram)
- theorists
- pragmatists
- activists
- reflectors
} not discrete categories

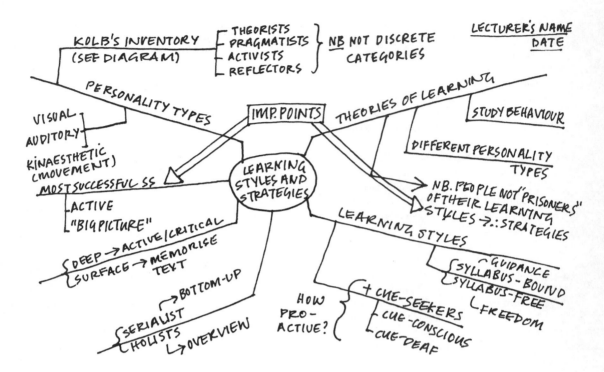

KOLB'S INVENTORY
(SEE DIAGRAM)

⌈ THEORISTS
⌊ PRAGMATISTS
⌈ ACTIVISTS
⌊ REFLECTORS

NB NOT DISCRETE
CATEGORIES

LECTURER'S NAME
DATE

PERSONALITY TYPES

IMP. POINTS

THEORIES OF LEARNING

STUDY BEHAVIOUR

VISUAL
AUDITORY
KINAESTHETIC
(MOVEMENT)
MOST SUCCESSFUL SS
ACTIVE
"BIG PICTURE"

LEARNING STYLES AND STRATEGIES

DIFFERENT PERSONALITY TYPES

NB. PEOPLE NOT "PRISONERS"
OF THEIR LEARNING
STYLES ∴ STRATEGIES

DEEP → ACTIVE/CRITICAL
SURFACE → MEMORISE TEXT

→ BOTTOM-UP
SERIALIST
HOLISTS
↳ OVERVIEW

HOW PRO-ACTIVE?

⌈ CUE-SEEKERS
⌊ CUE-CONSCIOUS
CUE-DEAF

LEARNING STYLES

GUIDANCE
SYLLABUS-BOUND
SYLLABUS-FREE
FREEDOM

Varieties of English

What does it mean to speak a language? When someone says *I can speak English* does that mean the same thing for everyone? It was once said of Britain and the United States that they are two countries divided by a common language. How can two countries be divided by having the same language? In this lecture I am going to talk about some of the things that can make the same language (specifically English, in this case) a source of distinctions and differences. In other words, I am going to talk about the varieties of English.

There are two main ways of looking at variety with reference to any given language. The first is how the language changes over time throughout its history, which could be over a period of several hundred years or longer. The second way is how a language varies at any particular point in time, for example the different varieties of English at this particular point in the 21st century. In this talk, I will start by very briefly saying something about the way English has changed throughout its history. Then I will come to my main topic, which is a quick look at some of the varieties of English in existence at the present point in time.

Let's start then by looking at variation in English over time. All languages change over time. Even within our own lifetime we will be aware that there are many words in common use today which either did not exist at all five or ten years ago, or which did exist but have taken on new meanings. Examples in English of fairly recent words include words like *dot-com* to mean a company or business that operates mainly through the Internet. Another new computer-related word is *cyberstalker*, meaning someone who stalks or harasses another person through the Internet. Not all new words are connected with new inventions. For example the verb *downsize* is a fairly recent new word: it means to reduce in size or scope, to become smaller. So you can speak of a business or a company *downsizing*, which may be a nice way of saying that it has sacked some of its workers.

Going back further in time, if you have ever read or seen the plays of Shakespeare, you will know that his 16th-century English (sometimes called Early Modern English) often has to be studied carefully before it can be fully understood. Some of the words he used have disappeared completely in the late modern English we use today. But even some of the words in his plays that look familiar have to be treated with care, because their meaning has changed. So, for example, the word *allow* which usually means 'to permit' today, in the 16th century could mean 'to approve'. A more striking example is the word *nice*. Today, to describe someone as 'nice' is to pay him or her a compliment, but in Shakespeare's day, *nice* could mean 'foolish'.

If we go back even further, say a thousand years, to Old English, we find that is so different from contemporary English that it has to be studied like a foreign language or else translated so that it can be understood. Historians of the English language often divide it into four periods: Old English (8th to the 11th centuries AD), Middle English (12th to the 15th centuries), Early Modern English (16th and 17th centuries) and Late Modern English (18th century to the present).

OK, let's come to the second part of this talk, which is concerned with varieties of English as it is used now. I am going to discuss contemporary varieties of English under two headings. First, there are varieties according to USER, that is according to the person who is speaking or writing. Secondly there are varieties according to USE, that is according to the purpose that the language is being used for, and the situation or circumstances in which it is being used.

Right, let's think of varieties according to user; let's think of the person using the language. When we are growing up, we imitate the variety of the language that we hear about us. This language will contain certain vocabulary items (lexical terms) and certain grammatical forms.

This variety of language according to vocabulary and grammar is called a DIALECT. In most languages there is usually one dialect that is spoken by all educated speakers of the language: this is called the STANDARD DIALECT.

As well as having certain words and grammatical forms, the language we learn as we grow up will also be pronounced in a certain way, be stressed in a certain way, and will be spoken with certain changes in tone-level or intonation. This variety according to pronunciation, stress and intonation is called an ACCENT. It is often the case that a particular dialect will be spoken with a corresponding accent. But not always. For example it often happens that a Standard Dialect will be spoken by educated speakers in different accents. In the UK, for – for instance, all educated people from Scotland, Ireland and Wales can speak Standard British English, but very often they will speak it with a distinctive Scottish, Welsh or Irish accent. Similarly in the United States an educated person from one of the Northern States will probably speak the same Standard American as someone from one of the Southern States, but there may be a marked difference in the accent.

Most languages have one standard dialect, but because English is such a widely spoken language several standard English dialects have emerged: I have already referred to British English and American English, but there is also, for example, Australian English, New Zealand English, Canadian English and South African English. There are also other dialects of English where it is widely used as a second language such as in India, Malaysia, Singapore, Hong Kong, West Africa and the West Indies, each with their own local vocabulary and grammatical terms not widely used elsewhere.

So we find that the part at the side of a street for pedestrians to walk on is called the *pavement* in Standard British English but the *sidewalk* in Standard American. Not only that but in the United States the word *pavement* can refer to any paved public thoroughfare, in other words, the street itself. To take another example, in Britain and in New Zealand, if a performance goes *like a bomb* it means it is a great success, whereas in Canada and the United States if a show *bombs*, it has been failure. So we can see how having a common language but using different dialects can on occasion lead to misunderstanding.

Now let us turn to varieties of English according to USE. The most obvious of these is the distinction between Spoken English and Written English, but there are others. The main point I want to make here is that when we are using English there is a variety of STYLES that we can choose from. Our choice of style is affected by various considerations, and we will now look at a few of these.

One important factor affecting the style of language we use depends on the relationships between the people who are communicating with each other. For example, people who know one another very well may use an INFORMAL style. People who are strangers or who wish to show deference, politeness or respect may use a more FORMAL style. So it might be that students will choose to address their teachers formally as Professor Smith or Doctor Jones, whereas one of their colleagues or friends will informally call them Tom or Mary, or whatever their first names are. However, formality may also be influenced by the situation. In a very formal situation even people who know one another very well may decide to use a more formal mode of speech when communicating.

The same rules apply to writing. In an informal letter, the writer may express gratitude by writing the word 'thanks' whereas in a more formal letter it might be considered more appropriate to use the phrase 'thank you'. However, the medium of communication usually does affect the style used. When sending e-mails and mobile phone text-messages, people often tend to use expressions and abbreviations that are not normal or even acceptable in other forms of written discourse.

OK, so far I've mentioned three things that can affect our choice of style. One is our relationship with the person we are speaking with or writing to. The second is the nature of the situation in which we are communicating, the context of communication, if you like. The third is the medium that we are using to communicate.

Now let us look at a fourth factor which can affect our style of discourse. This is the PURPOSE of the communication, what the language is being used for. An obvious example is the language of literature, and perhaps the clearest example here is the language of poetry. Poetry distinguishes itself from other forms of language in that it often uses rhyming words, it very often has a very regular rhythm, it often compares one thing to another by using simile or metaphor, or by using other special features of language like alliteration, when several words coming together begin with the same letter or sound. To take another example, the language of advertising often tries to attract our attention by using the same techniques as literature. It is not an accident that some of the most successful literary authors writing in English have worked at one time as copywriters for advertising agencies.

As students yourselves you will be familiar with the fact that every academic subject has its own specialised vocabulary – in fact you could almost say that knowing a subject means knowing how to use its specialised vocabulary. Obvious examples are medical terms, legal terms, the language of the various sciences like physics or biology and so on.

Apart from these specialised vocabularies, there is also a general academic way of speaking and writing which has been called Academic English. For example, in written academic English impersonal or passive forms are often used where otherwise we might prefer to use personal or active forms. So, in an academic paper you will often come across an expression like:

It was found that X happened

rather than:

I found that X happened **or** *We found that X happened.*

Another feature of Academic Discourse is the frequent use of hedging or qualifying expressions, such as:

It may well be the case that
According to these data
It seems likely that

These hedging or qualifying expressions are used because academic writers are usually careful not to make sweeping statements that can be disproved by discovering one exception. By the way, did you spot the way I hedged/ qualified that last sentence? I'll say it again, and see if you can spot the hedging word:

These hedging or qualifying expressions are used because academic writers are usually careful not to make sweeping statements that can be disproved by discovering one exception.

— · —

Yes. The hedging word was *usually*.

OK, I think it's time now to sum up the main points I've been trying to make in this talk. I hope I have given you enough examples to show that English, like the vast majority of other languages, is not one uniform unchanging thing. Firstly, it is continuously evolving and changing over time, so that we have several historical varieties of English, some of them so different from present-day English that they cannot be understood even by educated native speakers without careful study.

Secondly, there are many varieties of contemporary, present-day English. I have divided (em) these (eh) varieties (em) according to the identity of the USER (such as dialect and accent) and varieties according to USE, usually involving a conscious choice of style. We can vary our style, according to whom we are communicating with, the context or situation we are communicating in, the medium of communication we are using (speech, writing, e-mails, text messages etc.) and lastly the purpose of our communication, what we are using the language for.

[Mini-lecture – Outline notes]

a) Linear notes

VARIETIES OF ENGLISH
   ① ENGLISH OVER-TIME
   ② ENGLISH TODAY
① ENGLISH OVER TIME
     – NEW WORDS (dot-com/cyberstalker/downsize)
     – SHAKESPEARE (EARLY MODERN ENGLISH)
     e.g. allow = "approve", nice = "foolish"
     – 4 PERIODS
         (1) OLD ENGLISH
         (2) MIDDLE ENGLISH
         (3) EARLY MODERN E.
         (4) LATE MODERN E.
② ENGLISH TODAY
     – VARIETIES ACCORDING TO USER/USE
  (1) USER
     – DIALECT (VOCAB.+ GRAMMAR)
     – ACCENT (PRONUNCIATION ETC)
     – SEVERAL STANDARDS (US/UK/AUSTRALIA...)
     – ENGLISH AS A 2ND LANG.
  (2) USE
     – SPOKEN V. WRITTEN
     – CHOICE OF STYLE
        • RELATIONSHIPS (FORMAL/INFORMAL)
        • SITUATION
        • MEDIUM
        • PURPOSE
          – LITERATURE (POETRY)
          – ADVERTISING
          – ACADEMIC SUBJECTS
          – ACADEMIC ENGLISH
          (IMPERSONAL FORMS/HEDGING)

b) Branching notes

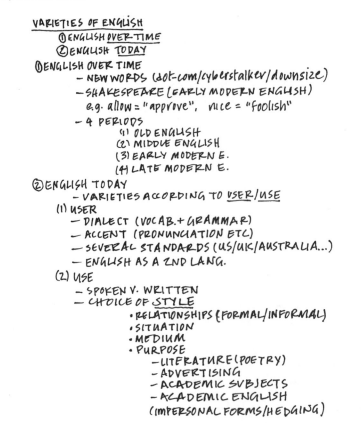
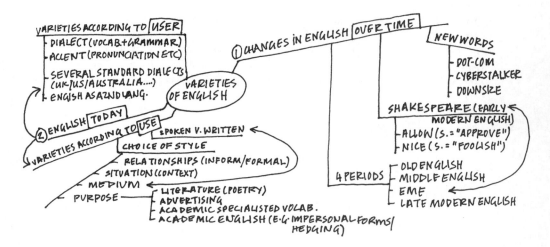

UNIT 3 Key

······················

TASK 1 **Preparing to research a topic (1)**

1–2 [See Figure 3.1]

······················

TASK 2 **Preparing to research a topic (2)**

1 Various answers. Some possible sub-topics are listed below. These are obviously only suggestions – many other answers are possible.

■ **The teaching of history in schools**

What is history FOR? [to learn from the mistakes of the past? / to instil national pride? / to promote understanding of other cultures? etc.];
What KIND of history should be taught? [national or international? / Is it about rulers or ordinary people? / Ancient or modern? / Political/Social/Economic/History of Science? etc.]; HOW should history be taught? [from a textbook? / from dictated notes? / using TV and film where possible?]; Is history a good thing? [does it reinforce national prejudices? / does it glorify battles and victories?]

■ **The usefulness of aid to developing countries**

Different KINDS of aid [international aid e.g. UNESCO / national government to government aid / aid from religious bodies / aid from private charities e.g. Save the Children]; arguments FOR [prevention of famine and disease / building up of a country's infrastructure (transport, education, water supply etc.) / voluntary way of transferring wealth from rich to poor]; arguments AGAINST [can undermine local industries, local enterprise / can make poor countries into the 'client states' of rich countries / can get countries into debt which they cannot repay / may not reach the poor people it is intended for; etc.]

■ **The issues raised by an expanding world population**

What is the nature of problem? [how many people are 'too many'? / will the world's population go on expanding at the present rate indefinitely? / are there already too many people?]; problems caused by over-population [pressure on food supplies / environmental pollution / using up of finite resources (e.g. energy)]; how to prevent overpopulation [compulsory or voluntary? / moral issues of contraception and abortion / role of education / cultural aspects of family planning]

■ **Equality of wealth in society**

How do you define 'rich' and 'poor'? Will the same definitions apply to all societies? Should there be an upper limit on income (wealth tax)? Should wealth be inherited by those who have not earned it, e.g. children of rich parents (inheritance tax)? What are the dangers of great differences of wealth in society? How should excellence and hard work be rewarded by society? How do societies become richer : by equalising wealth or by creating new wealth? How do you stop rich people from simply leaving the country?

2–3 Various answers

Identifying appropriate resources

1 Various answers. As far as 'Which would you turn to first?' is concerned, remember the golden rule is to start 'close to home', i.e. roughly in the order listed in the box 'Possible sources of information'.

Using keywords

Note: there are no uniquely correct strategies in using keywords. The following are suggestions which gave useful results for one researcher.

1 (*Amazonia*) Start with *deforestation*, then go on to *economic consequences of deforestation*, then add *Amazonia*.

2 (*economic growth*) Start with *economic growth*, then *high economic growth*, then add *problems*.

3 (*pressure groups*) Start with *pressure groups*, then go on to *pressure groups and political decision-making*.

4 (*population movement*) Start with *population movement*, then go on to *population movement from cities*, then add an appropriate city, e.g. *population movement from cities London*.

Using library resources

1 There are seven ways, by: Title; Author; Subject; Shelf mark (i.e. library number which indicates the location of the book on the library shelves); Journal Title; Keyword Search with Relevance (i.e. by entering key [important] words in the topic being searched, the results can be sorted by how relevant they are to the topic); Boolean Search (explained in the text).

2 a) The library seems to have 38 titles published within the last 10 years. Unless you are doing in-depth research it is unlikely that you will find the time to read all the titles. So careful selection is necessary!

b) They have been listed by date in descending order, i.e. with the most recent listed first. This might be useful, because more recent publications are often more relevant, and are obviously more up-to-date.

c) There is no 'right' answer to this task – it is really a matter of judgement. However, titles 2, 6, 7 and 8 would seem to be good titles to start with: they seem very relevant and seem to be broad in scope. Titles 4, 9, 5 and 2 also seem relevant but deal with more specialised sub-topics (effects of advertising on children [4, 9], the effect of TV on literacy [5] and the long-term effects of TV on children's later behaviour [2]).

Using library and computer-based resources

1 (*overlapping topics*) There is obvious overlap between *TV: Positive effects (evidence) / TV: Negative effects (evidence)* and all the other sub-topics. These two topics could provide the organising structure for the whole assignment.

2–3 (*Other tasks*) Various answers.

4 A sample answer to the last task, based on data provided by the first page of the Boolean search copied in Figure 3.3, follows.

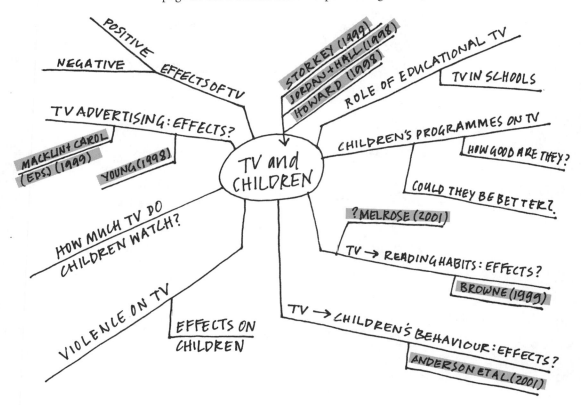

Brainstorming chart with potential sources added

⋮ ⋮ ⋮

TASK 7 Logging sources

1 Sources: Books

Keith F. PUNCH (2000)
Developing Effective Research Proposals
London: Sage Publications
Keywords: research proposals

Judith BELL (1999)

Doing Your Research Project: A guide for first-time

researchers in education and social science (3rd ed.)

Buckingham / Philadelphia: Open University Press

Keywords: research projects / education / social science

2 Sources: Journal articles

Peter K. SMITH, Monika SINGER, Helge HOEL and Cary L. COOPER (2003)

"Victimization in the school and the workplace: Are there any links?"

British Journal of Psychology 94:175–188

Keywords: victimization/school/workplace/bullying

TASK 8 Logging sources (annotated)
Various answers

TASK 9 Quoting and summarising (1)
1 Source note **A** is a summary whereas source note **B** contains a direct quotation.
2 **A**: The summary note gives an overview of the general theme of the text, and informs the reader about its conclusion. It might be useful for giving a reader a general idea about the message of this text.
   B: The quotation note concentrates on the conclusion and gives us the writer's own words. The quotation here has quite a lot of impact, so it might be useful to use the direct quotation to enliven a discussion of this topic.

TASK 10 Quoting and summarising (2)
1

Hazel MUIR and Betsy MASON

"Secret lives of dogs"

New Scientist, 3rd August 2002, p. 20

Keywords: animal cognition / dogs

2

> Researchers Robert Young and Rebecca West have devised an experiment which shows that it is not only some primates that can count: dogs also seem to have the same ability. (Muir and Mason, 2002:20)

3

> "Dogs [in an experimental situation] paid little attention when one plus one bowl resulted in two bowls...But they were confused when the experiment was manipulated to show that one plus one bowl appeared to equal three bowls, for example." (Muir and Mason, 2002:20)

4 Various answers

TASK 11 Exploiting sources

1 Various answers

2 a) *The purpose of references to Weinburg (1971), Weizenbaum (1984) and Kuiper (1992).* Charlton used these quotations to support his point that the early literature on over-zealous computing behaviour has tended to emphasise the negative aspects of such behaviour.

   b) *Quotation from Kuiper (1992).* In this quotation we see that Kuiper has introduced an interesting term to describe people who become over-involved with their computers: 'Space Cadets'. Charlton obviously wants to use this interesting term and then feels he has to quote from Kuiper to give an accurate definition of it.

   c) *(Moore, 1995 cited by Griffiths, 1998).* Charlton wants to show us that he is not quoting from the original source (Moore, 1995) but from a secondary source (Griffiths, 1998).

   d) *Young (1999) and Young (1996a).* These sources show that some researchers have discovered negative aspects of computer use not just among programmers (as in the sources quoted in §1) but also among students who have easy access to computers.

   e) *Agree/disagree.* Charlton agrees with his sources to the extent that over-zealous use of computers can lead to psychological and social problems. However, he also feels that the classification procedures adopted by some researchers have led them to overestimate the number of people who are 'addicted' to the use of computers.

f) *General use of sources.* In general, Charlton uses his sources to show that a certain point of view on computer addiction is widely held among those who have researched the topic. If this is so, it means that his own findings are more valuable, since they seem to challenge widely held beliefs.

TASK 12 Avoiding plagiarism

A ORIGINAL VERSION

1 (*threats*) Among the threats which Fukuyama envisages are: ability to control human behaviour through drugs for political rather than health or safety reasons; ability to prolong life (but not necessarily the *quality* of life) almost indefinitely; ability to breed children selectively for 'desirable' qualities, e.g. intelligence; interference with embryos for reasons which have nothing to do with the health or safety of the embryos; experiments/developments in biotechnology which offend against 'human dignity'.

2–3 various answers

B PLAGIARISED VERSION 1

4 Blatant plagiarism. Fukuyama's words and ideas have been used without acknowledgement.

C PLAGIARISED VERSION 2

5 Not so blatant, but still serious plagiarism. Although Fukuyama has been acknowledged as the source of these ideas, his words have been lifted without using quotation marks. The reader has no way of knowing exactly which of these thoughts are Fukuyama's and which come from the writer.

D PLAGIARISED VERSION 3

6 Serious plagiarism. Although some of Fukuyama's ideas are correctly attributed to him, not all of them are. There is nothing original from the writer in this paragraph, and the reader has no way of realising that.

Also, although it conveys Fukuyama's meaning, the quotation has been badly handled in that:
- Fukuyama's sentence did not begin with a lower-case letter (it started with a capital letter – 'We …'). Some academic styles allow this kind of minor change, but others do not
- the original sentence was written in italics
- the original sentence ended with the word *it* not *biotechnology*.

E ACCEPTABLE VERSION

7 Acceptable. The quotation is correctly handled. Using a colon allows the essay-writer to begin with the capital letter that is in the original. The reference of 'it' to 'biotechnology' is also explained, but the essay-writer has put this information in square brackets to show that it has been added to the quotation.

The essay-writer has also indicated that the sentence quoted was printed in italics in the original. It was not necessary to do this, but it is helpful to the writer's argument because the fact that Fukuyama has printed this point in italics shows that it is indeed 'a key point'.

The most important point to note is that, although the essay-writer is basically in agreement with Fukuyama's central thesis, Fukuyama's ideas have not just been 'cut and pasted' – they have been integrated into the writer's own argument, which is concerned with the importance of transparency in decision-making. The writer has used Fukuyama's insights, but has also added something original to the discussion. Whether readers will find the essay-writer's argument convincing is, of course, another issue.

UNIT 4 Key

TASK 1 **Topics, frames and assignment organisation**
(**Note:** frames are underlined.)

Assignment 1
a) <u>What factors would you identify in explaining why</u> women now make up nearly half of Britain's labour force?
b) Keywords: WOMEN/HALF/BRITAIN'S LABOUR FORCE
c) The question is looking for a LIST of REASONS.
d) You could use either the LIST pattern **C** or possibly the CAUSE/EFFECT pattern **D**.

Assignment 2
a) <u>Why</u> does scholastic achievement at school and university level vary between students from different social classes and ethnic backgrounds?
b) Keywords: SCHOLASTIC ACHIEVEMENT/SCHOOL AND UNIVERSITY/SOCIAL CLASSES/ETHNIC BACKGROUNDS.
c) The question is looking for an explanation. We will have to deal with two kinds of student (school/university) and two different variables (social class/ethnic background).
d) CAUSE/EFFECT: **D**

Assignment 3
a) <u>What evidence is there either to support or contradict the view</u> that the media have a powerful influence on audience beliefs?
b) Keywords: MEDIA/POWERFUL INFLUENCE/AUDIENCE BELIEFS
c) The question is looking for evidence for or against a particular point of view.
d) FOR/AGAINST: **B**

Assignment 4
a) <u>In what ways</u> are the patterns of immigration into Australia and the United States <u>similar and in what ways are they different?</u>
b) Keywords: PATTERNS OF IMMIGRATION/AUSTRALIA/UNITED STATES
c) We have to: (i) identify the patterns of immigration into Australia and the United States (what are they?); (ii) compare and contrast them.
d) COMPARE/CONTRAST: **F**

Assignment 5

a) <u>Give an account of</u> the legislative procedures by which new laws are enacted at national level in Malaysia.

b) Keywords: LEGISLATIVE PROCEDURES/NEW LAWS/NATIONAL LEVEL/MALAYSIA

c) We have to describe a process.

d) PROCESS DESCRIPTION: **A**

Assignment 6

a) Many industrially advanced countries have ageing populations. <u>Should something be done about this and, if so, what?</u>

b) Keywords: INDUSTRIALLY ADVANCED COUNTRIES/AGEING POPULATIONS

c) This question poses a problem and asks for a solution.

d) PROBLEM/SOLUTION: **E**

TASK 2 Process description: How a Compact Disc Hi-Fi Audio System works

Electronic systems are used to process *information*. Figure 4.2 shows a familiar example, a CD player and Hi-Fi system. For simplicity, only one channel is shown. A real system will handle stereo information and will have pairs of microphones, amps, and speakers, but apart from that the system behaves as shown.

When considering electronic systems we can talk about the information being carried around by some sort of varying signal voltage or current. This signal can be in various forms. For example, it can be an analog signal where the voltage/current level varies in proportion with the value we wish to carry. The CD system illustrated in Figure 4.2 uses both analog and digital signals.

The microphone produces an output voltage which changes in proportion with the varying air pressure falling upon it. These variations in voltage have the same pattern as those of the air pressure (i.e. the sound waves). For this reason the pattern of voltage fluctuations is said to be an analog of the sound pattern.

The voltage fluctuations produced by a normal microphone are very small. Hence they have to be enlarged with a suitable amplifier. In the Figure this is called a *pre-amp*. This name is used to indicate an amplifier placed at the 'front' of a system whose job is to boost weak signals up to a more useful level.

The amplified analog voltage pattern is then passed to a circuit which converts it into a stream of binary digits (1/0) which are converted into output as a pattern of high and low voltages representing the signal pattern of 1's & 0's. One of the most common choices (*TTL* or *Transistor-Transistor Logic*) uses any voltage in the range 3·5 Volts to 5·0 Volts as a '1' and anything from 0·5 Volts to 2·5 Volts as a '0'. Unlike analog signals, the precise digital voltage levels aren't usually important.

This flexibility about the exact voltage required is one of the main advantages of digital systems over analog ones. Slight changes in voltage don't change the actual information content of a digital signal but may ruin an analog pattern.

The digital pattern of information is recorded on the CD as a spiral pattern of pits which can be read by the CD player to recover the stream of binary 1's & 0's or bits. These are then converted back into the appropriate analog voltage pattern which is amplified and used to drive loudspeakers. These push and pull the air in the listening room to reproduce the sound-wave patterns originally recorded falling on the microphones.

Jim Lesurf (2003) *Scots Guide to Electronics* (Part 1, page 1). (The original text has been slightly edited.)

TASK 3 Comparing and contrasting

1 Minds/computers. (Sample answers)
  a) Three similarities: both can perform calculations; both can solve certain kinds of problems; both can 'communicate' (e.g. the Internet).
  b) Three differences: computers do not have emotions; computers are not creative in the way that humans are; computers are (in theory!) totally predictable – they can only react to the programs and data fed into them.

2–5 Various answers

TASK 4 Cause and effect

1 (Sample answers)
  a) Before gunpowder was invented, it was possible for a city to be safe from its enemies if it had a strong high wall. <u>This explains why</u> so many ancient cities were built with high walls around them.
  b) The land heats up more quickly than the sea and also cools more quickly. <u>As a result</u>, during the day, warm air over the land rises and cooler air from the sea blows onshore to take its place. At night, the land becomes cooler than the sea, so the winds tend to blow offshore, towards the sea.
  c) <u>One reason for</u> people leaving the countryside is possibly a lack of employment opportunities.

2–3 Various answers

TASK 5 For and against

1 a) (Frame <u>underlined</u>)
It has been suggested that all formal University examinations should be abolished, to be replaced by a system of continuous assessment by assignment. <u>How far would you be prepared to support such a proposal?</u> b) – f) Various answers

2 Various answers

TASK 6 Problem/solution

Various answers

TASK 7 Definition

Various answers

TASK 8 Evidence, implication and inference

1 various answers
2 a) (How do you think these data were obtained?) Probably by using questionnaires.
  b) Three most important qualities of a good lecture according to Arts students in:
    (i) *Cambridge*   delivery / interest / clarity
    (ii) *Leeds*   delivery / clarity / interest
    (iii) *Southampton* originality / clarity + interest

c) Three most important qualities of a good lecture according to Science students in:
   (i) *Cambridge*   clarity / delivery / notes
   (ii) *Leeds*   delivery + notes / interest
   (iii) *Southampton*   notes / clarity + comprehensibility
   (iv) *Northampton*   comprehensibility / grasp of subject / clarity

d) This information may not be generalisable to other universities and other countries because of differences in teaching and learning methods, and also perhaps cultural differences in attitudes to learning and teaching.

3 The main difference is the emphasis that Science students place upon the desirability of good notes. Also, the Science students in this sample were not nearly so interested in 'originality' as Arts students.

4 Various answers

TASK 9   Evaluating overall impact

1 The basic framework in this essay is FOR and AGAINST (Frame 4). It has this structure.
Argument for (1) (should be like primary and secondary education)
Argument for (2) (everyone benefits)
Argument for (3) (higher education is a human right)

Counter argument (1) (graduates earn more)
1st Refutation of c/a (not all graduates well-paid)
2nd Refutation of c/a (non-graduates can also be wealthy)
3rd Refutation of c/a (graduates have already been 'taxed')

Counter-argument (2) (will take studies more seriously)
Refutation of c/a (lazy students fail anyway)

So the body of the essay follows one of the models given, but there is no clear statement of the issues at the beginning and no summing-up at the end.

2 FIRST DRAFT
Tutor's comments

This is OK for a first draft, but there is a bit of scope for improvement.

I like the basic structure of your essay. As well as putting forward some reasonable arguments of your own, you have also taken on board possible opposing arguments and responded to them. (In a longer essay I would have expected some evidence from sources to back up your arguments about the supposed economic benefits of higher education and also the idea that higher education is a human right — what universities are FOR is a subject on which much ink has been spilled!)

The length of your essay is well inside the maximum length. It seems to me that this gives you plenty of scope to tackle the main problem I have with your essay, which is that it is inadequately "signposted". Although it has a reasonably good structure, that structure could be made clearer to the reader. I'd like you to work on that.

The language is fine. On a small stylistic point I thought that the repetition of "also" in the second paragraph could have been avoided.

I look forward to reading your final draft!

TASK 10   Improving overall impact

SECOND DRAFT

(NOTE: words in **bold** have been added. Words underlined have been deleted. Please note also that these drafts are examples: other acceptable versions are possible.)

Proposal for a graduate tax

In this essay I will argue against the introduction of a graduate tax on higher education. I will begin by stating the reasons for my opposition to such a tax. Then I will look at some of the arguments that have been put forward to justify this tax and give my reasons for rejecting them.

First, let me say why I find this suggestion unacceptable. I don't see why people should pay for higher education. After all, state primary and secondary education are free, why not state higher education? Anyway, **My first argument is economic.** It is in the country's interest to have all its citizens educated to the best of their ability. An educated workforce is the real wealth of a country. Everybody benefits from it, not just the ones who have been educated. If graduates have to repay the full cost of their fees, many clever people will be discouraged from going into higher education, and the whole country will suffer. **My second argument is a matter of principle**. Also, **A** university education is more than just a preparation for work. It is every citizen's human right to be freely educated according to their ability and their interests.

Now let us look at some of the arguments that have been advanced to justify this tax. Firstly, some people argue that graduates earn more than people who do not have degrees, and so they can afford to pay the extra graduate tax. But this is not fair. Not all the jobs that graduates do are well paid. Also there are many people who do not go to university, but go straight into a trade or into business and some of these people can end up being quite wealthy. Why should only the graduates be penalised? Also, graduates have already been "taxed" in a sense, because for many years they have not been able to earn the salaries they would have earned if they had gone straight into business after school.

Another **A second** argument for a graduate tax is that students will take their studies more seriously if they know they will eventually have to pay for them. But this argument is irrelevant. If students don't take their studies seriously, they will fail and never graduate, and so they won't pay the tax anyway.

To sum up, my rejection of this proposal is based on two key arguments: firstly, the fact that free higher education is to the economic benefit of the country, and secondly, the belief that free higher education for those who are capable of benefiting from it is in any case a basic human right.

FINAL DRAFT
(Note stylistic change (paragraph 3) in *italics*.)

Proposal for a graduate tax

In this essay I will argue against the introduction of a graduate tax on higher education. I will begin by stating the reasons for my opposition to such a tax. Then I will look at some of the arguments that have been put forward to justify this tax and give my reasons for rejecting them.

First, let me say why I find this suggestion unacceptable. I don't see why people should pay for higher education. My first argument is economic. It is in the country's interest to have all its citizens educated to the best of their ability. An educated workforce is the real wealth of a country. Everybody benefits from it, not just the ones who have been educated. If graduates have to repay the full cost of their fees, many clever people will be discouraged from going into higher education, and the whole country will suffer. My second argument is a matter of principle. A university education is more than just a preparation for work. It is every citizen's human right to be freely educated according to their ability and their interests.

Now let us look at some of the arguments that have been advanced to justify this tax. Firstly, some people argue that graduates earn more than people who do not have degrees, and so they can afford to pay the extra graduate tax. But this is not fair. Not all the jobs that graduates do are well paid. Also there are many people who do not go to university, but go straight into a trade or into business and some of these people can end up being quite wealthy. Why should only the graduates be penalised? *Further, it could be argued* that the graduates have already been "taxed" in a sense, because for many years they have not been able to earn the salaries they would have earned if they had gone straight into business after school.

A second argument for a graduate tax is that students will take their studies more seriously if they know they will eventually have to pay for them. But this argument is irrelevant. If students don't take their studies seriously, they will fail and never graduate, and so they won't pay the tax anyway.

To sum up, my rejection of this proposal is based on two key arguments: firstly, the fact that free higher education is to the economic benefit of the country, and secondly, the belief that free higher education for those who are capable of benefiting from it is in any case a basic human right. (428 words)

TASK 11 Proofreading a list of references
1 STYLE RULES

1 Authors' names are in strict alphabetical order.
2 Surname (family name) of first author is printed at the beginning of the reference.
3 First letter of surname is a capital letter (i.e. in upper case). The rest of the name is in lower case.
4 First names are indicated with initial letters only.
5 There is a full stop after each initial letter for the first names.
6 The date of publication is printed after the author's name, in brackets.
7 The date of publication is followed by a full stop (period).

8 If the publication is a book, the title is printed in *italics*, followed by a full stop.
9 If the reference is to a particular edition of a book, the number of the edition is printed after the title. There is no full stop between the title and the number of the edition. The edition is printed in ordinary type, in brackets, and the word *edition* is abbreviated to *ed.* (without a capital letter).
10 If the publication is an article or chapter of a book it is printed in normal type, but enclosed within single quotation marks.
11 If the article is taken from a collection of articles in an edited book, then it is followed by the word *in* followed by the names of the editors.
(**Note:** in many reference systems it is necessary also to give the actual page numbers of the article/chapter from a book; sometimes this information is given after the title, sometimes at the end of the reference. In the case of an article printed in a journal etc. the page numbers are always given.)
12 The editors' names are printed with the first name initials coming before the editors' surnames.
13 The abbreviation (Eds.) is put after the editors' names. This abbreviation is in brackets. It begins with a capital letter and ends with a full stop.
14 The title of a book is followed by the place of publication, followed by a colon, after which comes the name of the publisher.

2 **MISTAKES**
Malin – No place of publication (London)
Neal and Morgan – No Volume number, Issue number or page reference (16/1: 9–26)
Wrong alphabetical order. Two mistakes: (1) Fisher should come before Krause; (2) Saks should come after Neale
Witz – no date of publication (1992)

CORRECT VERSION
Coady, M. and Bloch, S. (Eds.) (1996). *Codes of Ethics and the Professions.* Victoria, Australia: Melbourne University Press.
Fisher, J., Gunz, S. and McCutcheon, J. (2001). 'Public/private interest and the enforcement of a code of professional conduct.' *Journal of Business Ethics*, 31/3: 191–208.
Krause, E.A. (1996). *Death of the Guilds: Professions, states and the advance of capitalism, 1930 to the present.* New Haven, Connecticut/London: Yale University Press.
Malin, N. (Ed.) (2000). *Professionalism, Boundaries and the Workplace.* London: Routledge.
Neal, M. and Morgan, J. (2000). 'The professionalization of everyone? A comparative study of the development of the professions in the United Kingdom and Germany.' *European Sociological Review*, 16/1: 9–26.
Saks, M. (1995). *Professions and the Public Interest: Medical power, altruism and alternative medicine.* London: Routledge.
Witz, A. (1992). *Professions and Patriarchy.* London: Routledge.

TASK 12 Drafting and re-drafting an assignment
Various answers

UNIT 5 Key

TASKS 1–6 Various answers

TASK 7 **Identifying terms that may have to be defined**

1 (Suggestions underlined)

a) <u>Democracy</u> is definitely the best way of running a country.

b) Scientists should be allowed to perform any kind of experiment they like: otherwise <u>progress</u> will come to a halt.

c) In this day and age, people cannot consider themselves <u>truly educated</u> unless they have studied a <u>scientific subject</u> in some depth.

d) The <u>urban (city-based) way of life</u> is obviously an <u>unnatural way of life</u>, and that is another reason why people should be discouraged from moving into the towns.

e) I think that everyone will agree that the first duty of a government is to ensure that everyone gets a <u>fair wage</u>.

f) The highest wages ought to be paid to those who actually do the work – in other words the members of <u>the working class</u>.

2 Various answers

TASK 8 **Establishing potentially useful evidence**

1 a) One member of the group knows a woman driver who is very careless and forgetful – *anecdotal evidence; unreliable – this particular woman may not be typical of women drivers in general.*

b) A comparison of the percentage of men drivers and women drivers found guilty of dangerous driving within a specific recent period – *useful statistical evidence, but not conclusive: the period in question may have been untypical; and the fact that people have not been apprehended by the police does not mean that they are safe drivers.*

c) The number of claims that women drivers make on their car insurance companies as compared to men drivers – *useful statistical evidence, but not conclusive: the fact of a claim leaves open the question of who was responsible for the incident that gave rise to the claim.*

2 a) Smoking cigarettes is bad for your health – *health statistics comparing smokers and non-smokers*

b) Hanging is a deterrent to murder (that is, some murders would not be committed if murderers knew they would be hanged if caught and found guilty) – *a comparison of murder rates between similar areas where one has the death penalty for murder and the other does not would be useful, but not conclusive – there might be other explanations for the differences between them.*

c) When workers go on strike, the reason given for the strike is usually a wage claim of some kind. But the real reason for most strikes is boring and unpleasant working conditions – *it would be useful to interview striking workers in depth to see how far their working conditions affected their decision to strike.*

d) The showing of violent scenes on TV and in films involving the use of guns is the reason for the increased use of guns by criminals these days – *psychological data on how people are affected by watching violence on TV would be relevant but not, of course, conclusive.*

TASKS 9 & 10 Various answers

UNIT 6 Key

TASK 1 School to University

Below are some possible comments.

- *Clubs.* It's not a good idea for Jim to cut himself off from sources of mental and physical relaxation. Of course, it's not a good idea to overdo these things either. There has to be a balance.
- *Work.* Jim seems to think that University 'work' consists of going to classes. The big difference between school and university is that in most subjects the work you do outside class is at least as important as that done in class and sometimes more so.
- '*The lecturers … give us very little guidance*'. If this is the case, it is up to Jim to be pro-active and to find out what he needs to know about the course. There should be course descriptions and previous examination papers available from the library; he should not be afraid to ask his tutors for information, and through the students' union it may be possible to contact more senior students who have done the course. There may also be a student counselling service that could help.
- *Time.* It sounds as though Jim has managed his time badly. He has to be more organised and systematic.
- *Giving up.* It's too early to give up. The question for Jim is: What is at the root of his lack of success? For example, does he still want to study these subjects? If not, are there other subjects he would prefer to study? He should discuss these issues with a course counsellor or sympathetic course tutor before rushing into a rash decision that he may regret later.

TASK 2 Differences in national university cultures

1 a) 'Traditional' teaching involves a very receptive kind of learning, which consists mostly of taking notes from lectures.
  b) (i) Both are quite traditional.
       Both use the same kind of teaching aids.
     (ii) IHK has much more informal staff–student relationships than WPI.
       IHK culture is generally more relaxed than WPI.
       IHK teaching groups are smaller, so tutors have a better chance of knowing students individually.
       IHK teachers are much more accessible.
       WPI students are more competitive because they have to pay for their tuition.

. . TASK 7 **Effects of revision**

1 a) Group A remembered most and Group E remembered least. The difference between these two groups was substantial: after about two months, Group A still remembered just under 40% of what they had learnt while Group E remembered less that 10%. The explanation for the difference seems to be that: (i) Group A was tested (and therefore encouraged to remember) almost immediately after learning, whereas Group E were not first tested until about 20 days later; (ii) Group A were given an extra test about 10 days after the first one.

   b) The best time for revising is immediately afterwards, for example straight after attending a lecture, taking part in a tutorial, reading a book or article.

   c) With Group A the rate of forgetting after the first test was quite steep (although from a higher base score from Group B, whose test was slightly later) but after the second test it slowed considerably. This shows the importance of regular frequent revision.

   d) Various answers

....
. . TASK 8 **Techniques for memorising**

1 There is a systematic progression in the numbers starting with the number at the bottom left-hand corner:
   $5 + 3 = 8$ $8 + 4 = 12$ $12 + 3 = 15$ $15 + 4 = 19$ (and so on).

2 Making a diagrammatic summary forces a learner to interact with what has to be learned and this helps both understanding and (therefore) memory. The diagram itself may make the content more easily remembered. Having the diagram on one page means the learner can take in the whole topic at a glance – this saves time and can give an 'overview' of the topic.

3 Various answers

....
. . TASK 9 **Thinking about exam preparation routines**
Various answers

Reading speed chart

Use the chart below to work out your reading speed for the named units. Note that the starting and finishing times given (in the left-hand column) are to the nearest quarter of a minute. Also please note that the columns are arranged according to increasing length of text, which is not necessarily the order in which the Tasks appear in the book. All times are in words per minute.

Time (mins/secs)	Task 5 (622 words)	Task 9 (740 words)	Task 10 (777 words)	Task 11 (830 words)	Task 6 (844 words)
1.00	622	740	777	830	844
15	498	592	622	664	675
30	415	493	517	553	562
45	355	422	444	474	482
2.00	311	370	389	415	422
15	276	328	345	369	375
30	249	296	311	332	338
45	226	269	282	301	307
3.00	207	246	259	277	281
15	191	228	239	255	260
30	178	211	222	237	241
45	166	197	207	221	225
4.00	156	185	194	208	211
15	146	174	183	195	198
30	138	164	172	184	188
45	131	156	164	175	178
5.00	124	148	155	166	169
15	118	141	148	158	160
30	113	135	141	151	153
45	108	129	135	144	147
6.00	104	123	130	138	141
15	100	118	124	133	135
30	96	114	120	128	130
45	92	110	115	122	125
7.00	88	105	111	119	121
15	85	102	107	114	116
30	83	97	104	111	113
45	80	95	100	107	109
8.00	*	92	97	103	106
15	*	90	94	101	102
30	*	87	91	98	99
45	*	85	89	95	96
9.00	*	82	86	92	94
15	*	80	84	90	91
30	*	*	82	87	89
45	*	*	80	85	87
10.00	*	*	*	83	84
15	*	*	*	81	82
30	*	*	*	*	80

Copyright sources

Unit 1, Tasks 3–4 Michael ARGYLE (2001), *The Psychology of Happiness* (2nd ed.) Hove, East Sussex: Routledge

Unit 1, Task 6 David CRYSTAL (2001), Adapted from *Language and the Internet* (CUP) (This article is a shortened version of an article which first appeared in the *SATEFL Newsletter* 21 (2) (Winter 2001): 5–7)

Unit 1, Task 7 David CRYSTAL (Ed.) 2000, *The Cambridge Encyclopedia* (4th ed.) CUP

Unit 1, Task 9 Lisa MELTON, His pain, her pain …*New Scientist*, 19.01.02: 32–35

Unit 1, Task 10 [No author], Never the twain shall meet …(Economics Focus feature article) *The Economist*, 02.02.02: 82

Unit 1, Task 11Extract from: Lester BROWN, Save the planet (and prosper) *The Ecologist* 31 (10), Dec 2001/Jan 2002: 26–31

Unit 2, Task 7 *Isaac ASIMOV (1971), *Twentieth Century Discovery* Macdonald and Jane's Ltd.

Unit 2, Task 14 Clark, D. (2000). (Diagram) *Learning Styles, How we go from the known to the unknown* On-line [08.03.03]: http://www.nwlink.com/~donclark/hrd/learning/styles,html 2

Unit 3, Figures 3.2, 3.3 University of Edinburgh Library

Unit 3, Figure 3.4 Google.com (2003)

Unit 3, Figure 3.5 Keith F PUNCH (2000), *Developing Effective Research Proposals*, London: Sage Publications

Unit 3, Figure 3.6 Judith BELL (1999), *Doing your Research Project* (3rd ed.), Buckingham: Open University Press

Unit 3, Task 9 David S LANDES (1999), [? – very brief extract] *The Wealth and Poverty of Nations* London: Abacus

Unit 3, Task 10 Hazel MUIR and Betsy MASON, Secret lives of dogs, *New Scientist*, 03.08.02: 20

Unit 3, Task 11 John P CHARLTON, A factor-analytic investigation of computer 'addiction' and engagement, *British Journal of Psychology*, 93(3): 329–344

Unit 3, Task 12 Francis FUKUYAMA (2003), [? – very brief extract] *Our Posthuman Future: Consequences of the biotechnology revolution*. London: Profile Books

Unit 4, Task 2 Jim LESURF, *The Scots Guide to Electronics*, Section "First 11", Part 1, pp. 1–2 e-mail: jcgl@st-and.ac.uk web site: http://www.standrews.ac.uk/~www_pa/Scots_Guide/ Retrieval path: www.ipl.org → subject collections → science and technology → electronics fi The Scots Guide to Electronics

Unit 4, Figure 4.3 THES Editorial © 2002, TSL Education Ltd. Online [26.03.02]: http://www.thes.co.uk/statistics/higher education/2000/first-year home gender.asp http://www.thes.co.uk/statistics/higher education/2000/first-year overseas gender.asp

Unit 4, Figure 4.5 *Peter MARRIS (1964), *The Experience of Higher Education*, Hove, East Sussex: Routledge and Kegan Paul, [? – very brief extract]

Unit 4, Task 10 *Publication Manual of the American , Psychological Association*, 4th Edition (1994). Washington, DC: APA.

Unit 6, Task 2 Erin GILSON, Cara OBADOWSKI and , John ROACH Educational cultures: A comparison of WPI versus IHK (Worcester Polytechnic Institute, USA, 2000) Online [28.01.03]: http://www.wpi.edu/Academics/Depts/IGSD/Perspectives/denmark2.html

Unit 6 Figure 6.3 *James DEESE (1964), *Principles of Psychology*. (Boston: Allyn & Bacon) H.F. SPITZER (1939). 'Studies in retention'. *Journal of Educational Psychology*, 30: 641–56.